Mastering OpenGL: From Basics to Advanced Rendering Techniques

OpenGL

Kameron Hussain and Frahaan Hussain

Published by Sonar Publishing, 2023.

While every precaution has been taken in the preparation of this book, the publisher assumes no responsibility for errors or omissions, or for damages resulting from the use of the information contained herein.

MASTERING OPENGL: FROM BASICS TO ADVANCED RENDERING TECHNIQUES

First edition. October 16, 2023.

Copyright © 2023 Kameron Hussain and Frahaan Hussain.

ISBN: 979-8223094050

Written by Kameron Hussain and Frahaan Hussain.

Table of Contents

8. Use Compute Shaders

9. Profile and Benchmark

10. Experiment and Iterate

11. Compiler Optimizations

12. Reduce Redundant Computations

13. Leverage GPU Features

14. Documentation and Profiling Tools

Section 18.4: Parallelism and Concurrency

1. Understanding Parallelism

2. Multi-threading for CPU Parallelism

3. GPU Parallelism

4. Thread Synchronization

5. Task Parallelism

6. Data Parallelism

7. Pipeline Parallelism

8. Asynchronous Execution

9. Optimizing for Parallelism

10. Concurrency Challenges

11. GPU Compute Frameworks

12. Hybrid Approaches

Section 18.5: Advanced Debugging Techniques

1. GPU Debugging Tools

2. Shader Debugging

3. Frame Debugging

4. Real-time Profiling

5. API Validation Layers

6. Capture and Replay

7. Remote Debugging

8. Instrumentation and Tracing

9. Memory Debugging

10. Crash Dumps and Minidumps

11. Code Analysis Tools

12. Community Resources

13. Continuous Integration (CI) and Testing

14. Documentation and Comments

Chapter 19: Cross-platform Considerations

Section 19.1: Porting to Mobile and Consoles

1. Platform-Specific APIs

2. Performance Optimization

3. Input Handling

Chapter 1: Advanced Shading Techniques

1.1 The Power of GLSL

In this section, we will delve into the fascinating world of GLSL (OpenGL Shading Language) and explore its capabilities in modern computer graphics. GLSL is a high-level shading language that allows us to create custom shaders for OpenGL applications. These shaders enable us to manipulate the rendering process, achieving impressive visual effects and realism in our graphics.

Understanding GLSL

GLSL is a C-like language specifically designed for GPU programming. It operates in parallel on the GPU's many cores, making it well-suited for tasks that require massive parallelism, such as real-time rendering. GLSL shaders can be used to control various stages of the rendering pipeline, including vertex shading, fragment shading, and geometry shading.

Here's a simple GLSL fragment shader that applies a grayscale filter to an image:

```glsl
#version 330 core

in vec2 texCoord;

out vec4 fragColor;

uniform sampler2D textureSampler;

void main() {

vec4 texColor = texture(textureSampler, texCoord);
```

```
float gray = dot(texColor.rgb, vec3(0.299, 0.587, 0.114));

fragColor = vec4(gray, gray, gray, texColor.a);

}
```

In this shader, we take advantage of GLSL's vectorized operations to efficiently compute the grayscale value of each pixel in real-time.

Shading Techniques

GLSL is a versatile tool that opens the door to various shading techniques. Some of the techniques we'll explore in this chapter include:

- **Normal Mapping**: Simulating fine surface details by perturbing surface normals.

- **Displacement Mapping**: Displacing vertices based on a height map for more intricate geometry.

- **Parallax Occlusion Mapping**: Creating the illusion of depth on textured surfaces.

- **Custom Shader Effects**: Developing unique visual effects tailored to your project's needs.

These techniques are essential for achieving realistic graphics in modern games and simulations. We'll dive deep into each of them, providing code examples and practical insights.

Why GLSL Matters

Understanding GLSL is crucial for graphics programmers, as it grants them the power to create stunning visuals and push the boundaries of what's possible in real-time rendering. Whether you're working on games, simulations, or any graphics-intensive application, mastering GLSL opens up a world of creative possibilities.

In the following sections, we'll embark on a journey through these advanced shading techniques, equipping you with the knowledge and skills to elevate your graphics programming to the next level. Let's begin by exploring the intricacies of normal mapping in Section 1.2.

Stay tuned for an exciting exploration of GLSL and its applications in modern computer graphics!

1.2 Normal Mapping

In this section, we'll delve into the concept of normal mapping, a powerful technique used in computer graphics to enhance the surface details and realism of 3D objects. Normal mapping is a form of texture mapping that allows us to simulate complex surface geometry without adding additional vertices to our models.

Understanding Normal Mapping

Normal mapping works by encoding per-pixel surface normals in a texture. These normals are used during rendering to perturb the shading calculations, creating the illusion of fine surface details and bumps on a flat model.

Let's take a look at the key components of a normal map:

- **RGB Values**: In a normal map texture, the RGB values represent the surface normals at each texel (texture pixel). The red channel typically represents the X-axis normal, the green channel represents the Y-axis normal, and the blue channel represents the Z-axis normal.

- **Normal Vector Transformation**: To use a normal map, we transform the RGB values from the [0, 1] range (common for texture data) to the [-1, 1] range (common for normal vectors). This transformation allows us to use the normals directly in lighting calculations.

Here's an example of what a portion of a normal map might look like:

// Sampled normal map texture

vec3 normalSample = texture(normalMap, texCoord).rgb;

// Transform the RGB values to normal vector

vec3 normal = normalize(normalSample * 2.0 - 1.0);

In this code snippet, we sample a normal from a texture, then transform its RGB values to a normal vector in world space.

Applying Normal Mapping

Normal mapping is typically applied in the fragment shader of a graphics pipeline. When rendering a pixel, we sample the normal from the normal map and use it to adjust the lighting calculations. This adjustment creates the appearance of bumps and fine details on the object's surface.

Here's a simplified example of how normal mapping can be applied in a fragment shader:

// Sampled normal map texture

```glsl
vec3 normalSample = texture(normalMap, texCoord).rgb;

// Transform the RGB values to normal vector

vec3 normal = normalize(normalSample * 2.0 - 1.0);

// Calculate lighting with the adjusted normal

vec3 lightDirection = normalize(lightPosition - fragmentPosition);

float diffuse = max(dot(normal, lightDirection), 0.0);

// Final color with normal mapping

vec3 finalColor = texture(diffuseTexture, texCoord).rgb * diffuse;
```

In this example, we adjust the lighting calculation by using the sampled normal from the normal map. This enhances the shading of the object, making it appear more detailed and realistic.

Benefits of Normal Mapping

Normal mapping is a valuable technique in computer graphics because it allows us to achieve high levels of detail with relatively low computational cost. It's particularly useful for adding surface imperfections, such as scratches, wrinkles, and bumps, to objects in a scene without the need for additional geometry.

In the next section, we'll explore another advanced shading technique: displacement mapping. Displacement mapping takes the concept of normal mapping further by physically displacing vertices to create intricate surface geometry.

1.3 Displacement Mapping

In this section, we'll dive into the fascinating world of displacement mapping, an advanced shading technique used to create intricate surface geometry in 3D objects. Displacement mapping takes the concept of normal mapping a step further by physically moving vertices based on a displacement map, allowing for the generation of detailed and complex surfaces.

Understanding Displacement Mapping

At its core, displacement mapping is about perturbing the position of vertices on a 3D model to create the illusion of additional geometry. Unlike normal mapping, which only affects lighting calculations, displacement mapping directly modifies the model's geometry, making it ideal for simulating fine surface details, such as wrinkles, grooves, or large-scale deformations.

The key component of displacement mapping is the displacement map itself. This map encodes height information that determines how much each vertex should be displaced along the surface normal. Higher values in the displacement map result in greater vertex displacement.

Here's a simplified example of how displacement mapping works:

```
// Sampled displacement map texture

float displacement = texture(displacementMap, texCoord).r;

// Displace the vertex along its normal

vec3 displacedPosition = vertexPosition + normal * displacement * scale;
```

In this code snippet, we sample the displacement value from a texture and use it to displace the vertex position. The scale factor controls the intensity of the displacement.

Applying Displacement Mapping

Displacement mapping is typically applied in the vertex shader of a graphics pipeline. When rendering a 3D object, each vertex's position is modified based on the values in the displacement map. This adjustment is performed before any lighting calculations, ensuring that the shading takes the modified geometry into account.

Here's a simplified example of how displacement mapping can be applied in a vertex shader:

```
// Sampled displacement map texture

float displacement = texture(displacementMap, texCoord).r;

// Displace the vertex along its normal

vec3 displacedPosition = vertexPosition + normal * displacement * scale;

// Output the displaced position

gl_Position = projectionMatrix * viewMatrix * vec4(displacedPosition, 1.0);
```

In this example, we calculate the displaced position for each vertex and transform it into clip space for rendering.

Benefits of Displacement Mapping

Displacement mapping offers several advantages in computer graphics:

- **Detail**: It allows for the creation of highly detailed surfaces without increasing the vertex count of a model. This is especially useful for close-up views or high-quality rendering.

- **Realism**: By physically displacing vertices, displacement mapping produces more realistic results than normal mapping, as it affects both shading and geometry.

- **Artistic Control**: Artists and developers have precise control over the level of detail and the shape of surface deformations, enabling them to achieve specific visual effects.

However, it's worth noting that displacement mapping can be computationally intensive, especially when dealing with a large number of vertices. Proper optimization and consideration of hardware capabilities are essential when implementing this technique.

In the next section, we'll explore another advanced shading technique: parallax occlusion mapping. Parallax occlusion mapping combines the principles of normal mapping and displacement mapping to create the illusion of intricate surface geometry while maintaining performance.

1.4 Parallax Occlusion Mapping

In this section, we'll explore the concept of parallax occlusion mapping, an advanced shading technique that combines the benefits of normal mapping and displacement mapping to create the illusion of highly detailed surface geometry while maintaining performance efficiency. Parallax occlusion mapping is particularly useful for adding intricate surface relief to objects in a scene.

Understanding Parallax Occlusion Mapping

Parallax occlusion mapping (POM) is an extension of normal mapping and displacement mapping. It simulates the effect of 3D depth on a 2D surface by sampling a height map and adjusting texture coordinates based on the perceived depth of the surface. This adjustment creates the illusion of depth and occlusion, making surfaces appear realistically contoured.

The key component of parallax occlusion mapping is the height map. This map encodes height information, just like a displacement map, but it doesn't physically displace vertices. Instead, it adjusts texture coordinates to create the appearance of depth.

Here's a simplified example of how parallax occlusion mapping works:

// Sampled height map texture

float height = texture(heightMap, texCoord).r;

// Calculate adjusted texture coordinates

vec2 parallaxTexCoord = texCoord + viewDirection.xy * height * scale;

// Sample the color texture using the adjusted coordinates

vec4 finalColor = texture(colorTexture, parallaxTexCoord);

In this code snippet, we sample the height from a texture and use it to calculate adjusted texture coordinates. These coordinates are then used to sample the color texture, creating the illusion of depth.

Applying Parallax Occlusion Mapping

Parallax occlusion mapping is typically applied in the fragment shader of a graphics pipeline. When rendering a pixel, we use the height map to adjust the texture coordinates before sampling the color texture. This adjustment makes it appear as though the surface has depth and relief.

Here's a simplified example of how parallax occlusion mapping can be applied in a fragment shader:

// Sampled height map texture

float height = texture(heightMap, texCoord).r;

// Calculate adjusted texture coordinates

vec2 parallaxTexCoord = texCoord + viewDirection.xy * height * scale;

// Sample the color texture using the adjusted coordinates

vec4 finalColor = texture(colorTexture, parallaxTexCoord);

// Output the final color

fragColor = finalColor;

In this example, we use the adjusted texture coordinates to sample the color texture, resulting in the final pixel color.

Benefits of Parallax Occlusion Mapping

Parallax occlusion mapping offers several advantages in computer graphics:

- **Detail**: It provides a high level of detail on surfaces, making them appear more realistic and visually appealing.

- **Performance**: Unlike displacement mapping, which physically moves vertices, parallax occlusion mapping is a screen-space effect, making it computationally efficient and suitable for real-time rendering.

- **Complexity**: It allows for the simulation of intricate surface details, such as bricks, tiles, or rocky terrain, without the need for additional geometry.

- **Artistic Control**: Artists and developers have control over the level of depth and the visual effect of surface relief, allowing for creative freedom.

In practice, parallax occlusion mapping is a valuable tool for achieving realistic surface details in games and simulations. However, it may require careful tuning and consideration of performance trade-offs to ensure optimal results in real-time applications.

In the next section, we'll explore another aspect of advanced shading: custom shader effects. Custom shader effects empower developers to create unique visual effects tailored to their project's specific requirements.

1.5 Custom Shader Effects

In this section, we'll explore the world of custom shader effects, where creativity meets technical expertise in computer graphics programming. Custom shader effects allow developers to go beyond the standard rendering techniques and create unique visual experiences tailored to the needs of their projects.

The Power of Custom Shaders

Custom shaders are a fundamental building block of modern computer graphics. They allow developers to write their own code that runs on the GPU, giving them complete control over how objects are rendered, shaded, and post-processed. This level of control is essential for achieving specific visual effects and artistic visions.

Custom shader effects can range from subtle enhancements to dramatic transformations of a scene. Some common use cases include:

- **Artistic Filters**: Applying artistic filters like sepia tones, grayscale, or stylized rendering to create a unique visual style.

- **Special Effects**: Implementing special effects such as heat distortion, underwater caustics, or stylized outlines to enhance the atmosphere of a game or simulation.

- **Material Simulation**: Simulating specific materials like glass, water, or metal by defining their optical properties and interaction with light.

- **Procedural Generation**: Generating procedural textures, landscapes, or patterns to create endless variations in game environments.

- **Post-processing**: Applying post-processing effects like bloom, motion blur, or depth of field to improve the overall visual quality.

Writing Custom Shaders

Custom shaders are typically written in shader languages like GLSL for OpenGL or HLSL for DirectX. These languages provide a set of functions and variables specifically designed for GPU programming.

Here's a simplified example of a custom shader effect in GLSL that applies a simple color shift:

```glsl
#version 330 core

in vec2 texCoord;

out vec4 fragColor;

uniform sampler2D textureSampler;

uniform vec3 colorShift;

void main() {

vec4 texColor = texture(textureSampler, texCoord);

fragColor = texColor + vec4(colorShift, 0.0);

}
```

In this shader, we take the input texture, sample its color at the specified texture coordinates, and add a color shift defined by the colorShift uniform variable.

Combining Custom Shaders

One of the powerful aspects of custom shaders is the ability to combine multiple shader effects to achieve complex visuals. This can be done through shader pipelines or by rendering objects with different shaders and blending their results.

For example, you could apply a custom shader that adds a water-like distortion effect to a scene and then combine it with a shader responsible for rendering reflections. This allows you to create realistic water surfaces with dynamic reflections.

Challenges and Optimization

While custom shaders offer immense creative freedom, they also come with challenges, such as performance optimization and compatibility across different GPUs. Optimizing shaders, managing resources efficiently, and handling edge cases are essential aspects of shader development.

Additionally, not all GPUs support the same shader features, so developers must consider fallback solutions or alternative techniques for compatibility.

In summary, custom shader effects are a powerful tool in the hands of graphics programmers and artists. They enable the creation of visually stunning and unique experiences in games, simulations, and other computer graphics applications. Whether you're aiming for realism or stylized visuals, custom shaders can help you achieve your vision.

Chapter 2: Geometry and Tessellation Shaders

2.1 Basics of Geometry Shaders

In this section, we'll delve into the fundamentals of geometry shaders, a key component of modern graphics pipelines. Geometry shaders allow for the dynamic generation and manipulation of geometry within the GPU, enabling a wide range of effects and optimizations.

What Is a Geometry Shader?

A geometry shader is a type of shader program that operates on the geometry of primitives (e.g., triangles, points, or lines) after they have been processed by the vertex shader. Unlike vertex shaders, which transform individual vertices, geometry shaders can create new vertices and primitives, modify existing ones, and even discard geometry based on user-defined conditions.

The primary tasks of a geometry shader include:

- **Creating New Geometry**: Geometry shaders can generate additional vertices and primitives. For example, they can turn a single input triangle into multiple output triangles, which is useful for tessellation or particle systems.

- **Modifying Geometry**: Geometry shaders can adjust the position, attributes, or other properties of existing vertices and primitives. This can be used for effects like displacement mapping or morphing.

- **Discarding Geometry**: Geometry shaders can selectively discard geometry based on certain conditions, effectively removing unwanted portions of a scene. This is useful for view frustum culling or level-of-detail (LOD) techniques.

Geometry Shader Stages

In the graphics pipeline, the geometry shader stage comes after the vertex shader and before the fragment shader. Here's an overview of the stages and their roles:

1. **Vertex Shader**: Transforms individual vertices into their final positions in clip space. It calculates attributes like position, normal, and texture coordinates.
2. **Geometry Shader**: Operates on primitive assemblies created by the vertex shader. It can generate new primitives or discard them as needed.
3. **Rasterization**: Converts the output of the geometry shader into fragments (pixels), taking into account how the primitives intersect with the screen pixels.
4. **Fragment Shader**: Calculates the final color and other attributes for each fragment, which are then blended to produce the pixel's color.

A Simple Geometry Shader Example

Here's a simple example of a geometry shader that takes input triangles and outputs wireframe lines:

```
#version 330 core

layout(triangles) in;

layout(line_strip, max_vertices = 6) out;
```

```
void main() {

for (int i = 0; i < gl_in.length(); i++) {

gl_Position = gl_in[i].gl_Position;

EmitVertex();

}

EndPrimitive();

}
```

In this shader, we specify that it takes input triangles and outputs lines (line_strip). It iterates over the input vertices, re-emitting them as output vertices, effectively creating wireframe lines.

Use Cases of Geometry Shaders

Geometry shaders have various practical use cases, including:

- **Tessellation**: Generating additional vertices to increase the geometric detail of surfaces.

- **Particle Systems**: Creating and controlling particles for special effects like smoke, fire, or sparks.

- **Procedural Geometry**: Generating complex procedural geometry such as trees, foliage, or rocky terrain.

- **Post-processing Effects**: Implementing screen-space effects like outline rendering or edge detection.

In the next sections, we'll explore more advanced aspects of geometry shaders, including their role in manipulating geometry on the fly and real-world applications in computer graphics.

2.2 Manipulating Geometry on the Fly

In this section, we'll delve into the fascinating world of manipulating geometry on the fly using geometry shaders. Geometry shaders provide a powerful tool for dynamically altering and creating geometry within the GPU, enabling a wide range of effects and optimizations.

Dynamic Geometry Generation

One of the most compelling capabilities of geometry shaders is the ability to generate new geometry on the GPU. This can be particularly useful when you need to create complex objects or add additional details to existing geometry without having to send new data from the CPU.

For example, consider a scenario where you want to render a field of grass with individual blades. Instead of storing and sending the position of each grass blade to the GPU, you can use a geometry shader to generate the blades from a single point or a grid of points. This significantly reduces the amount of data transferred between the CPU and GPU.

Procedural Geometry

Geometry shaders are often used for procedural geometry generation. Procedural generation allows you to create intricate and complex geometry by specifying rules and algorithms rather than explicitly defining every vertex. This approach is commonly used in games for generating terrain, foliage, and other natural or organic objects.

For instance, you can use a geometry shader to create a realistic rocky terrain by generating a mesh with varying heights, slopes, and rock formations based on a heightmap or procedural noise functions.

Particle Systems

Geometry shaders are well-suited for creating and controlling particle systems, which are commonly used for simulating effects like smoke, fire, sparks, and rain in games and simulations. With a geometry shader, you can emit and update particles directly on the GPU, resulting in efficient and visually appealing effects.

For example, a geometry shader can take a single point as input and emit multiple particles with different positions, velocities, and lifetimes. As the simulation progresses, the geometry shader can update the particle positions and adjust their attributes to simulate realistic particle motion.

Real-time Tessellation

Geometry shaders can also be used for real-time tessellation, a technique that dynamically subdivides and tessellates surfaces to add geometric detail based on the viewer's distance from the object. This is particularly useful for maintaining high-quality visuals while optimizing performance by reducing the level of detail for objects that are far from the camera.

Geometry shaders can generate additional vertices and primitives to enhance the detail of a surface as needed. For example, as the camera gets closer to a terrain surface, a geometry shader can add more vertices to represent fine details in the landscape.

A Practical Example

Here's a simple example of a geometry shader that generates additional points on a grid, effectively creating a particle system:

```glsl
#version 330 core

layout(points) in;

layout(points, max_vertices = 100) out;

uniform float time;

void main() {

// Emit 100 points in a circular pattern

for (int i = 0; i < 100; i++) {

float angle = float(i) * 6.2831853 / 100.0;

vec4 position = gl_in[0].gl_Position + vec4(cos(angle) * 0.2, sin(angle) * 0.2, 0.0, 0.0);

gl_Position = position;

EmitVertex();

}

EndPrimitive();

}
```

In this shader, a single input point is transformed into 100 points arranged in a circular pattern. This demonstrates how geometry shaders can generate new geometry based on predefined rules.

Performance Considerations

While geometry shaders offer tremendous flexibility, they can also be performance-intensive, especially when generating large amounts of geometry. It's essential to optimize and carefully manage the workload of geometry shaders to ensure smooth rendering performance.

In the next section, we'll explore more advanced applications of geometry shaders and their role in real-world graphics programming scenarios.

2.3 Introduction to Tessellation

In this section, we'll introduce the concept of tessellation in computer graphics and its significance in modern rendering pipelines. Tessellation is a technique that enables the dynamic subdivision of primitive surfaces into smaller, more detailed segments, allowing for the representation of complex and highly detailed objects.

What Is Tessellation?

Tessellation is the process of subdividing a primitive, such as a triangle or a quad, into a grid of smaller primitives. This grid can then be used to represent surfaces with varying levels of detail. The primary goal of tessellation is to improve the visual fidelity of rendered objects by adding geometric detail where needed.

Tessellation can be divided into three key stages:

1. **Tessellation Control Shaders (TCS)**: These shaders determine how the original primitive should be subdivided. They take user-defined control points and

output tessellation factors that influence the tessellation process.

2. **Tessellation Evaluation Shaders (TES)**: These shaders calculate the positions of the newly generated vertices based on the tessellation factors. They are responsible for interpolating the control points to create the final tessellated vertices.

3. **Geometry Shaders (GS)**: While not always necessary, geometry shaders can be used to further process the tessellated geometry. They can add additional vertices, perform culling, or apply other transformations.

Key Benefits of Tessellation

Tessellation offers several key benefits in computer graphics:

- **Adaptive Detail**: Tessellation allows for the adaptive subdivision of surfaces, ensuring that areas of interest receive more detail while distant or less important regions have fewer vertices. This adaptive approach helps optimize performance while maintaining visual quality.

- **Smooth Curvature**: Tessellation can create smooth, curved surfaces, making it well-suited for modeling organic objects, characters, and terrain.

- **Realistic Terrain**: In terrain rendering, tessellation can be used to create realistic landscapes with fine details, such as rocky cliffs, crevices, and natural erosion features.

- **Dynamic Level of Detail (LOD)**: Tessellation enables dynamic LOD adjustments, ensuring that objects maintain their quality even as they move closer or farther from the camera.

Tessellation Control and Evaluation Shaders

The tessellation process relies on tessellation control shaders (TCS) and tessellation evaluation shaders (TES). These shaders work together to control and generate the tessellated vertices.

Here's a simplified example of a tessellation control shader:

```glsl
#version 430 core

layout(vertices = 3) out;

void main() {

// Output tessellation levels based on distance to the camera

gl_TessLevelOuter[0] = 4;

gl_TessLevelOuter[1] = 4;

gl_TessLevelOuter[2] = 4;

gl_TessLevelInner[0] = 4;

}
```

In this example, the tessellation control shader sets the tessellation levels based on the distance to the camera. Higher levels of tessellation are used when objects are closer to the camera, providing more detail.

The tessellation evaluation shader, which follows the TCS, calculates the positions of the tessellated vertices:

```glsl
#version 430 core

layout(triangles, equal_spacing, cw) in;
```

```
void main() {

// Calculate the final vertex position using interpolation

vec3 p0 = gl_in[0].gl_Position.xyz;

vec3 p1 = gl_in[1].gl_Position.xyz;

vec3 p2 = gl_in[2].gl_Position.xyz;

vec3 position = gl_TessCoord.x * p0 + gl_TessCoord.y * p1 + gl_TessCoord.z * p2;

// Output the final position

gl_Position = vec4(position, 1.0);

}
```

In this example, the tessellation evaluation shader uses barycentric coordinates (gl_TessCoord) to interpolate the positions of the tessellated vertices within the original triangle.

Tessellation in Real-world Applications

Tessellation is widely used in various graphics applications, including video games, simulations, architectural visualization, and more. It plays a critical role in rendering highly detailed environments and characters, making scenes appear more lifelike and immersive.

In gaming, tessellation is employed for terrain rendering, character modeling, and water surfaces. It allows developers to strike a balance between performance and visual quality, ensuring that players can explore rich and detailed game worlds.

Tessellation also finds applications in non-real-time rendering, such as in the creation of high-quality pre-rendered animations, visual effects, and architectural visualizations.

In the next sections, we'll explore advanced tessellation techniques, adaptive tessellation, and practical use cases in real-time graphics programming.

2.4 Adaptive Tessellation Techniques

In this section, we'll delve into adaptive tessellation techniques, a critical aspect of tessellation that enables surfaces to be subdivided dynamically based on factors like screen space error, distance from the camera, or other criteria. Adaptive tessellation ensures that geometric detail is allocated efficiently to maintain visual quality while optimizing performance.

The Need for Adaptive Tessellation

While tessellation offers the advantage of adding detail to surfaces, it can become computationally expensive when applied uniformly to all objects in a scene. In many cases, not all parts of a surface require the same level of detail. For example, distant objects can be tessellated less densely than objects close to the camera, and smooth areas may need fewer tessellated vertices than regions with high curvature.

Adaptive tessellation addresses this issue by dynamically adjusting the level of detail based on criteria that make sense for a particular scene or object. This results in more efficient GPU usage, reduces unnecessary vertex processing, and ensures that computational resources are allocated where they matter most.

Screen Space Error

One common approach to adaptive tessellation is based on screen space error. Screen space error measures how much a tessellated triangle deviates from its projected size on the screen. The idea is to tessellate a triangle further if its projected size on the screen exceeds a certain error threshold.

Here's a simplified example of a tessellation control shader using screen space error:

```glsl
#version 430 core

layout(vertices = 3) out;

uniform mat4 projectionMatrix;

uniform float maxScreenSpaceError;

void main() {

// Calculate the projected vertices

vec4 p0 = projectionMatrix * gl_in[0].gl_Position;

vec4 p1 = projectionMatrix * gl_in[1].gl_Position;

vec4 p2 = projectionMatrix * gl_in[2].gl_Position;

// Calculate the screen space area of the triangle

float area = length(cross(p1.xyz - p0.xyz, p2.xyz - p0.xyz));

// Set tessellation levels based on screen space error

float maxArea = maxScreenSpaceError * maxScreenSpaceError;

gl_TessLevelOuter[0] = sqrt(area / maxArea);
```

```glsl
gl_TessLevelOuter[1] = sqrt(area / maxArea);

gl_TessLevelOuter[2] = sqrt(area / maxArea);

gl_TessLevelInner[0] = sqrt(area / maxArea);

}
```

In this shader, we calculate the screen space area of the triangle and set tessellation levels based on the error threshold (maxScreenSpaceError). Triangles that project larger than this error threshold are tessellated further to reduce error.

Distance-based Tessellation

Another common approach to adaptive tessellation is based on distance from the camera. Objects that are closer to the camera require more detail, while distant objects can have coarser tessellation.

Here's a simplified example of a tessellation control shader using distance-based tessellation:

```glsl
#version 430 core

layout(vertices = 3) out;

uniform mat4 modelViewProjectionMatrix;

uniform float maxTessDistance;

void main() {

// Calculate the distance from the camera to the triangle

vec3 cameraPosition = vec3(0.0, 0.0, 0.0); // Camera position in world space
```

```
vec4 centroid = (gl_in[0].gl_Position + gl_in[1].gl_Position +
gl_in[2].gl_Position) / 3.0;

vec3 trianglePosition = (modelViewProjectionMatrix *
centroid).xyz;

float distance = length(trianglePosition - cameraPosition);

// Set tessellation levels based on distance

gl_TessLevelOuter[0] = maxTessDistance / distance;

gl_TessLevelOuter[1] = maxTessDistance / distance;

gl_TessLevelOuter[2] = maxTessDistance / distance;

gl_TessLevelInner[0] = maxTessDistance / distance;

}
```

In this shader, we calculate the distance from the camera to the triangle's centroid and set tessellation levels based on the maximum tessellation distance (maxTessDistance). Closer objects receive higher tessellation levels.

Benefits of Adaptive Tessellation

Adaptive tessellation techniques offer several benefits in computer graphics:

- **Efficient Resource Usage**: Adaptive tessellation ensures that computational resources are used efficiently, allocating more detail where it matters most and reducing processing for distant or less important objects.

- **Improved Performance**: By dynamically adjusting the level of detail, adaptive tessellation can significantly improve rendering performance, especially in scenes with a mix of close and distant objects.

- **Consistency**: Adaptive tessellation helps maintain a consistent level of detail across a scene, preventing objects from appearing overly tessellated or too coarse.

- **Visual Quality**: Visual quality is enhanced as adaptive tessellation allocates detail to regions that are more likely to be visible or contribute to the scene's realism.

In practice, adaptive tessellation is a valuable tool for optimizing rendering pipelines in games, simulations, and other graphics applications. It allows developers to strike a balance between performance and visual quality, resulting in smoother and more efficient graphics rendering.

2.5 Real-World Applications

In this section, we'll explore real-world applications of geometry and tessellation shaders in computer graphics. These shaders play a crucial role in creating immersive and visually stunning environments in games, simulations, and other graphics-intensive applications.

Terrain Rendering

Geometry and tessellation shaders are frequently used in terrain rendering. They enable the creation of realistic landscapes with varying levels of detail. By dynamically tessellating the terrain mesh based on the viewer's distance and perspective, developers can maintain high-quality visuals without sacrificing performance.

Terrain shaders can simulate complex terrain features such as rocky cliffs, mountain ranges, valleys, and rivers. They can also incorporate techniques like texture splatting, where multiple textures are blended to create rich and detailed terrain surfaces.

Character Modeling and Animation

Geometry shaders are essential for character modeling and animation in video games and animated films. They allow for the creation of characters with smooth, realistic curves and surfaces. Tessellation shaders can dynamically adjust the level of detail on character models, ensuring that facial features, clothing, and other details appear sharp when viewed up close.

Additionally, tessellation shaders are used in cloth simulations to provide realistic cloth behavior. Cloth simulation relies on dynamically tessellated meshes that respond to forces such as wind and gravity, creating lifelike animations for characters' clothing.

Water and Fluid Simulation

Water rendering in games and simulations often utilizes geometry and tessellation shaders to achieve realistic water surfaces. Geometry shaders can generate waves and ripples on the water's surface, while tessellation shaders ensure that the water mesh adapts to the viewing distance.

Fluid simulations, such as those used for smoke, fire, and liquids, also benefit from geometry and tessellation shaders. These shaders can generate and manipulate particle systems that simulate the behavior of fluids, creating visually convincing effects.

Level of Detail (LOD) Techniques

Geometry and tessellation shaders play a pivotal role in implementing LOD techniques to optimize rendering performance. LOD is crucial for maintaining a consistent frame rate in complex scenes with a mix of objects at varying distances from the camera.

By using geometry shaders, developers can dynamically reduce the complexity of distant objects by simplifying their geometry. This process is known as "geometry LOD." Tessellation shaders can then be employed to add detail to objects as they move closer to the camera, ensuring a smooth transition between LOD levels.

Architectural Visualization

In architectural visualization and design, geometry shaders are employed to create detailed 3D models of buildings, interiors, and landscapes. These shaders facilitate the rendering of realistic architectural elements, such as intricate facades, interior furnishings, and landscaping features.

Tessellation shaders are used to adaptively tessellate architectural models, ensuring that fine details are present when examining the design up close. This level of detail is essential for architects, designers, and clients to visualize and assess architectural projects accurately.

Dynamic Effects and Particles

Geometry shaders are instrumental in the creation of dynamic effects and particle systems. These shaders can generate and manipulate particles on the GPU, enabling the simulation of effects like sparks, smoke, fire, and explosions.

By utilizing geometry shaders, developers can efficiently create and render large numbers of particles with various behaviors and appearances. Tessellation shaders can be applied to achieve smooth transitions between different particle states, making particle systems appear seamless and realistic.

Artistic Stylization

Geometry and tessellation shaders also find applications in artistic stylization. These shaders allow artists and designers to create unique visual styles, such as cel shading or stylized outlines. By manipulating geometry and tessellating surfaces creatively, developers can achieve visually striking and distinctive aesthetics in their projects.

In summary, geometry and tessellation shaders are versatile tools that enhance the visual quality and performance of computer graphics in a wide range of applications. From terrain rendering and character modeling to fluid simulations and architectural visualization, these shaders contribute to the creation of immersive and captivating digital experiences.

Chapter 3: Advanced Texturing

3.1 Multitexturing Techniques

In this section, we'll explore multitexturing techniques, a fundamental concept in computer graphics that allows us to apply multiple textures to surfaces. Multitexturing is a powerful tool for adding realism, detail, and complexity to objects in games, simulations, and 3D applications.

The Basics of Multitexturing

Multitexturing involves the simultaneous application of multiple textures to a single object or surface. Each texture is blended or combined in some way to produce the final color of a pixel. This technique is essential for achieving various visual effects, including realistic material representation, terrain texturing, and more.

The core idea of multitexturing is to assign multiple texture units to a shader program, each representing a different texture. These textures can be sampled independently and then combined using blending or other operations. The resulting color contributes to the final pixel color.

Texture Units and Samplers

In modern graphics APIs like OpenGL and DirectX, multitexturing is achieved using texture units and samplers. Texture units represent individual texture slots that can be bound to specific textures, while samplers are used to access these textures within shaders.

Here's a simplified example of how texture units and samplers are used in an OpenGL shader:

```glsl
#version 330 core

uniform sampler2D texture1; // Sampler for the first texture

uniform sampler2D texture2; // Sampler for the second texture

in vec2 texCoord; // Texture coordinates provided by the vertex shader

out vec4 fragColor; // Final fragment color

void main() {

// Sample the first texture

vec4 color1 = texture(texture1, texCoord);

// Sample the second texture

vec4 color2 = texture(texture2, texCoord);

// Blend the two colors (e.g., using alpha blending)

fragColor = mix(color1, color2, 0.5); // Blend with equal weight

}
```

In this example, we have two texture units (texture1 and texture2) that are sampled using the texture function. The colors from these textures are blended using the mix function with equal weight to create the final fragment color.

Use Cases of Multitexturing

Multitexturing serves various purposes in computer graphics:

- **Material Realism**: In 3D rendering, multitexturing is used to simulate complex materials like wood, marble, or brick. Multiple textures representing different material properties (e.g., diffuse color, normal map, specular reflection) are combined to achieve realistic surface appearance.

- **Terrain Rendering**: In terrain rendering, multitexturing is crucial for creating detailed landscapes. Different textures are blended based on height, slope, or other criteria to represent various terrain features like grass, rocks, and snow.

- **Decals and Detail Textures**: Multitexturing is employed to add small-scale details to surfaces, such as decals (e.g., graffiti on walls) or detail textures (e.g., scratches on metal surfaces).

- **Layered Textures**: It's used to layer textures on top of each other, allowing artists and designers to create intricate patterns and effects by combining textures with different transparencies and blending modes.

- **Masking and Blending**: Multitexturing is often used for masking and blending operations. For example, it can be used to create realistic reflections on water surfaces by blending a reflection texture with the scene based on the Fresnel factor.

Advanced Techniques in Multitexturing

Multitexturing can be combined with advanced techniques to achieve even more compelling results:

- **Normal Mapping**: Multitexturing is often used in conjunction with normal mapping to simulate fine surface details without the need for high-polygon models.

Normal maps can be combined with diffuse textures to enhance the appearance of surfaces.

- **Parallax Mapping**: Parallax mapping, also known as offset mapping, uses multitexturing to create the illusion of depth and relief on flat surfaces. Multiple textures are sampled at different heights to create the appearance of 3D geometry.

- **Procedural Texturing**: Multitexturing can be combined with procedural textures to create dynamic and infinite variations in textures. Procedural textures can simulate patterns like clouds, marble, or wood grain.

- **Texture Atlases**: Texture atlases are collections of smaller textures packed into a single large texture. Multitexturing is used to access specific regions of the atlas, enabling efficient rendering of numerous objects with shared textures.

In summary, multitexturing is a versatile and essential technique in computer graphics that enables the creation of detailed and realistic surfaces. Whether used for simulating materials, rendering terrain, or adding intricate details, multitexturing enhances the visual quality of 3D environments and objects.

3.2 Texture Atlas

In this section, we'll explore the concept of a texture atlas, which is a technique commonly used in computer graphics to optimize the rendering of multiple textures by packing them into a single large texture. Texture atlases are especially useful when dealing with a large number of small textures, such as those used for game objects, characters, or terrain.

What Is a Texture Atlas?

A texture atlas is a single texture that contains multiple smaller textures, arranged in a grid or another pattern. Each smaller texture, often referred to as a "subtexture" or "sprite," occupies a specific region within the atlas. These subtextures can then be accessed and rendered individually as needed.

Texture atlases are widely used in real-time graphics because they offer several advantages:

- **Reduced Texture Bindings**: In graphics APIs like OpenGL or DirectX, changing textures (i.e., binding a new texture) can be a costly operation. Texture atlases minimize the number of texture switches, which can significantly improve rendering performance.

- **Efficient GPU Memory Usage**: Combining multiple textures into a single atlas reduces the overall memory footprint compared to storing each texture separately. This is especially beneficial when targeting devices with limited GPU memory.

- **Faster Rendering**: Accessing a texture atlas is often faster than accessing multiple separate textures because the former can be cached more efficiently by the GPU.

Creating a Texture Atlas

Creating a texture atlas typically involves several steps:

1. **Texture Packing**: Arrange individual textures into a grid

within the atlas texture. The packing algorithm must ensure that subtextures do not overlap and that the atlas size is optimized to minimize wasted space.

2. **Mapping Coordinates**: Assign texture coordinates to vertices in your 3D models or 2D sprites to specify which region of the atlas to sample. These coordinates are often referred to as "UV coordinates."

3. **Texture Sampling**: In the shader, use the UV coordinates to sample from the atlas texture. By adjusting the UV coordinates, you can select different subtextures from the atlas.

Texture Atlas Implementation

Here's a simplified example of how to implement a texture atlas in OpenGL:

#version 330 core

uniform sampler2D atlasTexture; // *Sampler for the texture atlas*

in vec2 texCoord; // *UV coordinates passed from the vertex shader*

out vec4 fragColor; // *Final fragment color*

void main() {

// *Adjust UV coordinates to sample from a specific subtexture in the atlas*

vec2 subtextureOffset = vec2(0.25, 0.0); // *Example offset for the second subtexture*

vec2 adjustedTexCoord = texCoord + subtextureOffset;

// *Sample from the atlas texture using adjusted UV coordinates*

```
vec4 color = texture(atlasTexture, adjustedTexCoord);

// Output the sampled color

fragColor = color;

}
```

In this example, we assume that the atlas texture contains four subtextures arranged in a 2x2 grid. The shader adjusts the UV coordinates based on the subtexture offset to sample a specific subtexture from the atlas.

Use Cases of Texture Atlases

Texture atlases are employed in various scenarios in computer graphics:

- **Sprite Sheets**: In 2D games, sprite sheets often use texture atlases to store multiple frames of animations for characters and objects.

- **Font Rendering**: When rendering text in games and applications, a font atlas is often used to store characters and symbols.

- **Optimizing Game Assets**: For 3D games, texture atlases help optimize the rendering of game objects, characters, and environments by reducing texture switches.

- **GUI Elements**: Graphical user interfaces (GUIs) frequently use texture atlases to store icons, buttons, and other interface elements.

- **Mobile and Web Development**: In mobile and web development, texture atlases can be used to optimize texture loading and rendering, particularly for WebGL applications.

Texture atlases are an efficient solution for managing and rendering multiple textures in real-time graphics, making them a valuable tool for improving rendering performance and resource management in a wide range of applications.

3.3 Cube Maps and Skyboxes

In this section, we'll explore cube maps and skyboxes, two essential techniques in computer graphics used for rendering realistic and immersive environments, especially in 3D games and simulations.

Cube Maps

A cube map is a texture consisting of six individual 2D textures arranged to form the faces of a cube: one for each face (front, back, left, right, top, and bottom). Cube maps are primarily used to simulate reflections, refractions, and environment mapping in 3D scenes.

Cube maps are generated by capturing the environment from a specific point, such as a camera or a reflective surface, and storing the images from each direction into the corresponding cube map faces. These cube maps can then be used as textures in shaders to simulate various effects.

Cube Map Creation

Creating a cube map typically involves capturing six images from a specific point of view and arranging them into the cube map format. Here's a simplified example of generating a cube map in OpenGL:

```
// Create an empty cube map texture

GLuint cubemapTexture;

glGenTextures(1, &cubemapTexture);

glBindTexture(GL_TEXTURE_CUBE_MAP, cubemapTexture);

// Load and assign each face of the cube map

for (GLuint i = 0; i < 6; ++i) {

// Load and assign the image for each cube map face

// Example: Load and assign the front face

glTexImage2D(GL_TEXTURE_CUBE_MAP_POSITIVE_X + i,

0, GL_RGB, width, height, 0, GL_RGB, GL_UNSIGNED_BYTE, data);

}

// Set cube map parameters (e.g., filtering, wrapping)

glTexParameteri(GL_TEXTURE_CUBE_MAP,
GL_TEXTURE_MIN_FILTER, GL_LRINEAR);

glTexParameteri(GL_TEXTURE_CUBE_MAP,
GL_TEXTURE_MAG_FILTER, GL_LINEAR);
```

```
glTexParameteri(GL_TEXTURE_CUBE_MAP,
GL_TEXTURE_WRAP_S, GL_CLAMP_TO_EDGE);

glTexParameteri(GL_TEXTURE_CUBE_MAP,
GL_TEXTURE_WRAP_T, GL_CLAMP_TO_EDGE);

glTexParameteri(GL_TEXTURE_CUBE_MAP,
GL_TEXTURE_WRAP_R, GL_CLAMP_TO_EDGE);
```

Cube Map Usage

Once created, cube maps are applied in shaders to simulate various effects. Common uses include:

- **Environment Mapping**: Cube maps can be used to simulate reflections and refractions on 3D objects. The reflection vector from the camera is used to sample the cube map, producing realistic reflective surfaces.

- **Skyboxes**: Cube maps are often used to create skyboxes, which provide a backdrop to the 3D scene. A skybox cube map is mapped onto a cube surrounding the camera, creating the illusion of a distant environment.

Skyboxes

A skybox is a technique used to create a realistic and immersive background for a 3D scene, typically representing distant scenery or an environment. Skyboxes are often employed in video games and simulations to provide a sense of space and depth.

Skyboxes are created using a cube map texture or a set of individual textures for each face of the surrounding cube. The cube is placed at the camera's position, ensuring that it always surrounds the viewer.

When rendering, the 3D scene is drawn in the center of the cube, and the cube map is used as the background.

Creating a Skybox

Creating a skybox involves setting up the cube and applying the skybox texture. Here's a simplified example of creating and rendering a skybox in OpenGL:

```
// Create a skybox VAO (vertex array object) and VBO (vertex buffer object)

GLuint skyboxVAO, skyboxVBO;

glGenVertexArrays(1, &skyboxVAO);

glGenBuffers(1, &skyboxVBO);

glBindVertexArray(skyboxVAO);

glBindBuffer(GL_ARRAY_BUFFER, skyboxVBO);

glBufferData(GL_ARRAY_BUFFER, sizeof(skyboxVertices), &skyboxVertices, GL_STATIC_DRAW);

// Set up shaders and load skybox texture

// ...

// Render the skybox

glBindVertexArray(skyboxVAO);

glBindTexture(GL_TEXTURE_CUBE_MAP, cubemapTexture); // Use the cube map texture

glDrawArrays(GL_TRIANGLES, 0, 36);
```

glBindVertexArray(0);

Usage of Skyboxes

Skyboxes serve various purposes in 3D graphics:

- **Atmosphere and Ambiance**: Skyboxes contribute to the atmosphere and ambiance of a scene, providing a visually appealing and immersive background.

- **Bounding the Scene**: Skyboxes help bound the 3D scene, preventing the viewer from seeing beyond the scene's boundaries.

- **Realism**: In outdoor scenes, skyboxes enhance realism by simulating distant terrain, buildings, or natural landscapes.

- **Reflections**: In some cases, skyboxes can be used to provide reflections in water or reflective surfaces when cube maps are not available or practical.

In summary, cube maps and skyboxes are vital techniques in computer graphics for creating immersive and realistic environments. Cube maps are versatile for simulating reflections and refractions, while skyboxes enhance the overall ambiance of 3D scenes and serve as visually engaging backgrounds. When used effectively, these techniques contribute to the visual quality and immersion of games, simulations, and virtual environments.

3.4 Texture Compression

In this section, we'll delve into texture compression, a technique used in computer graphics to reduce the memory footprint of textures while preserving visual quality. Texture compression is essential for optimizing the storage and performance of graphics applications, especially in scenarios where memory resources are limited.

Why Texture Compression?

Texture compression addresses two critical concerns in computer graphics:

1. **Memory Efficiency**: Uncompressed textures can consume a significant amount of GPU memory, especially when dealing with high-resolution textures or large texture atlases. Texture compression reduces the memory requirements of textures, enabling the use of more textures within the available memory budget.
2. **Bandwidth Reduction**: When textures are transferred from system memory to GPU memory or between GPU memory and shaders, bandwidth can become a bottleneck. Compressed textures reduce the amount of data transferred, improving rendering performance, particularly in situations where texture streaming is involved.

Common Texture Compression Formats

Several texture compression formats are commonly used in graphics APIs, such as OpenGL and DirectX:

- **DXT (DirectX Texture Compression)**: DXT is a family of block-based texture compression formats widely used in DirectX applications. DXT formats include DXT1, DXT3, and DXT5, each offering varying levels of compression and visual quality.

- **ETC (Ericsson Texture Compression)**: ETC is a texture compression format primarily used in OpenGL applications, particularly on mobile platforms. ETC formats include ETC1 and ETC2, which provide varying levels of compression and support for transparency.

- **ASTC (Adaptive Scalable Texture Compression)**: ASTC is a modern texture compression format that offers a wide range of compression options. It is highly versatile, providing both high compression ratios and high visual quality, making it suitable for a variety of devices and platforms.

Compressing and Decompressing Textures

Texture compression involves two main operations: compression and decompression. Compression takes place offline during asset creation, where the original texture is converted into a compressed format. Decompression occurs at runtime when the texture is needed for rendering.

Here's a simplified example of how to compress and decompress a texture using the ASTC format in OpenGL:

Compression (Asset Creation)

// Load the original texture

GLuint originalTexture;

// Load the texture...

// Create a compressed texture

GLuint compressedTexture;

glGenTextures(1, &compressedTexture);

glBindTexture(GL_TEXTURE_2D, compressedTexture);

// Use a library or tool to compress the original texture into ASTC format

// This is typically done offline during asset preparation

// Upload the compressed texture to GPU memory

// glCompressedTexImage2D(...);

__Decompression (Runtime)__

// Bind the compressed texture

glBindTexture(GL_TEXTURE_2D, compressedTexture);

// The GPU automatically decompresses the texture when sampled in shaders

Trade-offs in Texture Compression

While texture compression offers significant benefits, it comes with trade-offs:

- **Visual Quality**: Higher compression ratios may result in noticeable artifacts, especially in textures with fine details or sharp edges. Choosing the appropriate compression format and settings is essential to balance quality and memory savings.

- **Runtime Decompression**: Decompressing textures at runtime consumes GPU resources and can introduce latency. However, modern GPUs are designed to handle decompression efficiently.

• **Compatibility**: Different platforms and GPUs support varying texture compression formats. Developers must consider compatibility when choosing compression formats for their applications.

In conclusion, texture compression is a crucial technique in computer graphics for optimizing memory usage and improving rendering performance. It allows graphics applications to use high-quality textures while minimizing memory requirements and bandwidth usage. Careful selection of compression formats and settings is necessary to strike the right balance between memory savings and visual quality.

3.5 Procedural Texturing

In this section, we'll explore the concept of procedural texturing, a technique used in computer graphics to generate textures algorithmically rather than using pre-existing image data. Procedural texturing offers several advantages, including flexibility, scalability, and the ability to create complex and unique textures at runtime.

What Is Procedural Texturing?

Procedural texturing involves the generation of textures through mathematical algorithms and functions. Instead of relying on static image files, procedural textures are created on-the-fly within shaders or other code. This approach allows developers to generate textures dynamically, making them well-suited for various scenarios.

Advantages of Procedural Texturing

Procedural texturing offers several key benefits:

- **Flexibility**: Procedural textures can be customized and modified at runtime, enabling dynamic changes to a scene's appearance. This flexibility is valuable for creating interactive and adaptive environments.

- **Resolution Independence**: Procedural textures are resolution-independent, meaning they can be used at any resolution without loss of quality. This is particularly useful for scaling textures to different display sizes and screen resolutions.

- **Small Memory Footprint**: Procedural textures require minimal memory because they are generated on-the-fly rather than loaded from image files. This makes them suitable for platforms with limited memory resources.

- **Infinite Variation**: Procedural textures can produce an infinite variety of patterns and details, making them suitable for generating natural phenomena like clouds, terrain, and procedural noise.

Procedural Texture Generation

Procedural textures are created through mathematical functions and algorithms that define the texture's appearance. Some common techniques and algorithms used in procedural texturing include:

- **Perlin Noise**: Perlin noise is a widely-used algorithm for generating natural-looking patterns such as clouds, marble, and terrain. It is characterized by smooth, organic shapes and is often used as a basis for more complex textures.

- **Worley Noise (Voronoi Diagrams)**: Worley noise, also known as Voronoi diagrams, is used to create irregular cell patterns. It is employed in applications like terrain generation, procedural landscapes, and organic textures.

- **Fractal Patterns**: Fractal algorithms like the Mandelbrot set and fractal Brownian motion (fBm) are used to create self-similar and recursive patterns. These algorithms can produce intricate and complex textures.

- **L-System**: L-systems are used to generate plant-like structures, including branching trees and foliage. They are commonly used in game environments to create realistic vegetation.

Using Procedural Textures in Shaders

Procedural textures are typically implemented within shaders, allowing for real-time texture generation and rendering. Shaders use mathematical functions to calculate the color and properties of each pixel in a procedural texture.

Here's a simplified example of a fragment shader in GLSL that generates a procedural texture:

```glsl
#version 330 core

in vec2 texCoord; // Texture coordinates from vertex shader

out vec4 fragColor; // Final fragment color

void main() {
```

// Calculate the color of the procedural texture based on texCoord

vec3 color = vec3(texCoord.x, texCoord.y, 0.5);

// Output the color

fragColor = vec4(color, 1.0);

}

In this example, the procedural texture's color is determined by the texCoord, which represents the texture coordinates. The shader generates a simple gradient-like pattern based on the texCoord.

Use Cases of Procedural Texturing

Procedural texturing finds applications in various areas of computer graphics:

- **Terrain Generation**: Procedural textures are used to create realistic terrain, including the generation of heightmaps, terrain features, and ground cover.

- **Cloud Rendering**: Cloud patterns in the sky can be generated procedurally, allowing for dynamic and realistic cloud formations.

- **Natural Phenomena**: Procedural textures are employed to simulate natural phenomena such as fire, smoke, water, and weather effects.

- **Artistic Effects**: Procedural texturing enables the creation of artistic and stylized visual effects, including abstract patterns and artistic rendering techniques.

- **Performance Optimization**: Procedural textures can be used to reduce memory usage and increase performance by generating textures on-the-fly rather than storing them in memory.

In summary, procedural texturing is a versatile technique in computer graphics that allows for the dynamic and flexible generation of textures. Whether used for terrain generation, natural phenomena, artistic effects, or performance optimization, procedural textures offer a powerful tool for creating unique and engaging visuals in games, simulations, and other graphics applications.

Chapter 4: Post-processing and Effects

4.1 Introduction to Post-processing

In this section, we will introduce the concept of post-processing and its significance in computer graphics. Post-processing refers to a set of techniques applied to rendered images after they have been generated by the graphics pipeline. These techniques can enhance the visual quality of a scene, add various effects, and improve the overall aesthetic of a game or application.

The Role of Post-processing

Post-processing plays a crucial role in computer graphics for several reasons:

1. **Visual Enhancement**: Post-processing can dramatically improve the visual appeal of a scene by applying color correction, contrast adjustments, and other enhancements that make the image more vibrant and realistic.
2. **Special Effects**: Many visual effects, such as motion blur, depth of field, and bloom, are achieved through post-processing. These effects add realism and cinematic quality to games and simulations.
3. **Performance Optimization**: Some post-processing techniques can optimize performance by reducing the computational load on the graphics hardware. For example, reducing the number of rendered frames or simplifying geometry can improve performance without sacrificing visual quality.
4. **Artistic Style**: Post-processing allows developers to define a specific artistic style for their games or applications. By

applying filters and adjustments, developers can create unique visual identities.

Common Post-processing Techniques

Several common post-processing techniques are used in computer graphics:

- **Depth of Field (DOF)**: DOF simulates the way a camera lens focuses on objects, blurring objects in the foreground or background to create a sense of depth. It is commonly used in rendering to emphasize the main subject.

- **Motion Blur**: Motion blur simulates the blurring effect of objects in motion. It adds realism to fast-moving objects and can enhance the cinematic feel of a game.

- **Bloom**: Bloom creates a halo or glow around bright objects in the scene, giving them a luminous appearance. This effect is often used to simulate intense light sources or add a dreamy ambiance.

- **Color Grading**: Color grading involves adjusting the colors and tones of an image to achieve a specific look or mood. It is widely used in film and game development to set the visual tone of a scene or game.

- **Anti-aliasing**: Anti-aliasing techniques are used to reduce the jagged and pixelated edges in rendered images. This results in smoother and more visually pleasing graphics.

Implementing Post-processing

Post-processing effects are typically implemented using shaders, specifically fragment shaders. These shaders take the final rendered image as input, manipulate its pixels, and produce the post-processed output.

Here's a simplified example of a post-processing shader in GLSL that applies a grayscale filter to the input image:

```glsl
#version 330 core

in vec2 texCoord; // Texture coordinates from the vertex shader

out vec4 fragColor; // Final fragment color

uniform sampler2D inputTexture; // Input rendered image

void main() {

// Sample the input image

vec4 color = texture(inputTexture, texCoord);

// Convert color to grayscale

float gray = dot(color.rgb, vec3(0.299, 0.587, 0.114));

color.rgb = vec3(gray);

// Output the post-processed color

fragColor = color;

}
```

In this example, the fragment shader samples the input image and converts it to grayscale. The resulting color is then output as the post-processed image.

Post-processing Frameworks

Developers often use post-processing frameworks and libraries to simplify the implementation of post-processing effects. These frameworks provide a range of built-in effects and tools for creating custom post-processing shaders.

In summary, post-processing is a fundamental aspect of computer graphics that enhances the visual quality and realism of rendered scenes. It allows for the application of various effects, from basic enhancements to complex cinematic effects, and plays a significant role in defining the visual style of games and applications.

4.2 Depth of Field Implementation

Depth of Field (DOF) is a post-processing effect commonly used in computer graphics to simulate the way cameras focus on objects, creating a sense of depth and realism in rendered images. In this section, we will explore the implementation of Depth of Field and its significance in enhancing visual quality.

Understanding Depth of Field

Depth of Field refers to the range of distances in a scene that are in focus. In real-world photography and cinematography, DOF is controlled by adjusting the camera's aperture and focal length. Objects within the DOF range appear sharp, while those outside it are progressively blurred.

In computer graphics, DOF is achieved through post-processing, where the rendering pipeline calculates the blur based on the distance between objects and the camera's focal point.

Components of DOF

To implement Depth of Field, several components need to be considered:

1. **Focal Point**: The point in the scene where the camera is focused. Objects at this distance will be in sharp focus.
2. **Aperture Size**: Similar to a camera, the virtual aperture size controls how much light enters the camera. A wider aperture (lower f-stop) results in a shallower DOF.
3. **Blur Strength**: Determines the strength of the blur applied to objects outside the DOF. Stronger blur creates a more pronounced DOF effect.
4. **Foreground and Background Objects**: Objects in front of or behind the focal point will be progressively blurred based on their distance from the focal point.

Depth of Field Algorithm

The Depth of Field effect is typically implemented in a post-processing shader. Here's a simplified example of how to implement DOF in a fragment shader:

```glsl
#version 330 core

in vec2 texCoord; // Texture coordinates from the vertex shader

out vec4 fragColor; // Final fragment color

uniform sampler2D colorTexture; // Input rendered image
```

uniform sampler2D depthTexture; // *Depth map*

uniform float focalDistance; // *Focal distance*

uniform float apertureSize; // *Aperture size*

uniform float blurStrength; // *Blur strength*

void main() {

// *Sample the depth value of the current fragment*

float depth = texture(depthTexture, texCoord).r;

// *Calculate the blur factor based on depth and focal distance*

float blurFactor = abs(depth - focalDistance) * apertureSize;

// *Apply blur to the fragment color*

vec3 blurredColor = texture(colorTexture, texCoord + blurFactor).rgb;

// *Blend the blurred color with the original color based on blur strength*

vec3 finalColor = mix(texture(colorTexture, texCoord).rgb, blurredColor, blurStrength);

// *Output the final color*

fragColor = vec4(finalColor, 1.0);

}

In this shader, we sample the depth value of the current fragment and calculate the blur factor based on the difference between the fragment's depth and the focal distance. The blur is then applied to the fragment color, and the final color is obtained by blending the blurred color with the original color based on the blur strength.

Configuring Depth of Field

Configuring Depth of Field involves adjusting the parameters in the shader, such as the focal distance, aperture size, and blur strength. These parameters can be controlled interactively to achieve the desired DOF effect in real-time applications.

Depth of Field is a valuable post-processing effect in computer graphics that enhances the realism and visual quality of rendered scenes. It is commonly used in video games, simulations, and film production to create cinematic and immersive visuals.

4.3 Motion Blur and Anti-aliasing

In this section, we'll explore the concepts of motion blur and anti-aliasing, two post-processing techniques that enhance the visual quality of rendered images in computer graphics.

Motion Blur

Motion blur is a post-processing effect used to simulate the blurring of objects in motion, replicating the way a camera captures fast-moving objects in the real world. It adds realism and a cinematic quality to rendered scenes, especially in scenarios involving high-speed movement.

Implementation of Motion Blur

Implementing motion blur in a post-processing shader involves capturing multiple frames of the scene and blending them together to create the illusion of motion. The key components of motion blur include:

- **Velocity Information**: To determine the amount of blur for each pixel, you need to know the velocity (speed and direction) of objects in the scene. This information is often stored in a separate velocity buffer or rendered as a G-buffer.

- **Temporal Accumulation**: Over several frames, accumulate the color values of each pixel based on the object's velocity. The more frames you accumulate, the stronger the motion blur effect.

Here's a simplified example of how to implement motion blur in a fragment shader:

```glsl
#version 330 core

in vec2 texCoord; // Texture coordinates from the vertex shader

out vec4 fragColor; // Final fragment color

uniform sampler2D colorTexture; // Input rendered image

uniform sampler2D velocityTexture; // Velocity buffer

uniform float motionBlurAmount; // Motion blur strength

void main() {

// Sample the velocity information

vec2 velocity = texture(velocityTexture, texCoord).xy;

// Calculate the blur offset based on velocity
```

```glsl
vec2 blurOffset = -velocity * motionBlurAmount;

// Accumulate color over several frames to create motion blur

vec4 blurredColor = vec4(0.0);

for (int i = 0; i < NUM_SAMPLES; ++i) {

vec2 offset = texCoord + i * blurOffset;

blurredColor += texture(colorTexture, offset);

}

blurredColor /= float(NUM_SAMPLES);

// Output the final blurred color

fragColor = blurredColor;

}
```

In this shader, we sample the velocity information, calculate the blur offset based on the velocity, and accumulate color values over multiple frames to create the motion blur effect.

Anti-aliasing

Anti-aliasing is a technique used to reduce the jagged and pixelated edges (aliasing) in rendered images, resulting in smoother and more visually pleasing graphics. It addresses the inherent limitations of digital rendering, where lines and edges may not align perfectly with the pixel grid.

Implementing Anti-aliasing

Anti-aliasing is typically implemented by taking multiple samples per pixel and averaging the colors to reduce pixel-level artifacts. The key components of anti-aliasing include:

- **Multisampling**: Multisampling is a common anti-aliasing technique where multiple samples are taken within each pixel. These samples are used to determine the final pixel color.

- **Filtering**: To reduce aliasing artifacts, apply filtering techniques such as bilinear filtering, trilinear filtering, or anisotropic filtering. These techniques smooth out textures and improve image quality.

Here's a simplified example of how to implement multisample anti-aliasing (MSAA) in a fragment shader:

```glsl
#version 330 core

in vec2 texCoord; // Texture coordinates from the vertex shader

out vec4 fragColor; // Final fragment color

uniform sampler2DMS colorTexture; // Multisampled color texture

void main() {

// Sample the multisampled color texture

vec4 finalColor = vec4(0.0);

for (int i = 0; i < NUM_SAMPLES; ++i) {
```

```
finalColor += texelFetch(colorTexture, ivec2(texCoord *
textureSize(colorTexture)), i);

}

finalColor /= float(NUM_SAMPLES);

// Output the final anti-aliased color

fragColor = finalColor;

}
```

In this shader, we sample the multisampled color texture and average the colors to obtain the anti-aliased result.

Significance of Motion Blur and Anti-aliasing

Motion blur and anti-aliasing are essential techniques in computer graphics for improving visual quality and realism:

- **Motion Blur**: Motion blur adds realism to fast-moving objects and enhances the cinematic feel of a scene. It is commonly used in video games and simulations to create a sense of speed and action.

- **Anti-aliasing**: Anti-aliasing reduces the visual artifacts caused by aliasing, resulting in smoother edges and more polished graphics. It is crucial for delivering high-quality visuals in games and applications.

Both motion blur and anti-aliasing contribute to the overall aesthetic and immersion of computer-generated scenes, making them valuable tools in the field of computer graphics.

4.4 Color Grading and Correction

In this section, we'll delve into color grading and correction, two post-processing techniques used in computer graphics to adjust and enhance the colors and tones of rendered images. These techniques play a crucial role in defining the visual style and mood of a game or application.

Color Grading

Color grading is the process of altering the colors and tones of an image to achieve a specific look, mood, or artistic style. It is widely used in film production and game development to create unique visual identities for scenes or entire games.

Implementation of Color Grading

Color grading is implemented using lookup tables, also known as color grading or color correction maps (LUTs or CCMs). These maps map input colors to desired output colors, allowing for a wide range of color transformations.

Here's a simplified example of how to apply color grading in a fragment shader using a 2D texture as a color grading lookup table:

```glsl
#version 330 core

in vec2 texCoord; // Texture coordinates from the vertex shader

out vec4 fragColor; // Final fragment color

uniform sampler2D colorTexture; // Input rendered image

uniform sampler2D colorGradingLUT; // Color grading lookup
table
```

```glsl
void main() {
// Sample the color from the input image

vec4 inputColor = texture(colorTexture, texCoord);

// Sample the color grading LUT

vec4 gradedColor = texture(colorGradingLUT, inputColor.rgb);

// Output the final graded color

fragColor = gradedColor;

}
```

In this shader, we sample the input color from the rendered image and use it as a lookup value in the color grading LUT to obtain the final graded color.

Color Correction

Color correction is the process of adjusting the colors of an image to ensure accurate and consistent color representation. It corrects for colorimetric inaccuracies caused by factors such as lighting conditions, camera sensors, and display devices.

Implementation of Color Correction

Color correction is implemented using color matrices or algorithms that adjust the color channels (red, green, and blue) of an image. It aims to achieve color fidelity and ensure that colors appear as intended.

Here's a simplified example of how to apply color correction in a fragment shader using a color correction matrix:

```glsl
#version 330 core

in vec2 texCoord; // Texture coordinates from the vertex shader

out vec4 fragColor; // Final fragment color

uniform sampler2D colorTexture; // Input rendered image

uniform mat4 colorCorrectionMatrix; // Color correction matrix

void main() {

// Sample the color from the input image

vec4 inputColor = texture(colorTexture, texCoord);

// Apply color correction using the matrix

vec4 correctedColor = colorCorrectionMatrix * inputColor;

// Output the final corrected color

fragColor = correctedColor;

}
```

In this shader, we sample the input color and apply the color correction matrix to obtain the final corrected color.

Significance of Color Grading and Correction

Color grading and correction are essential techniques in computer graphics for several reasons:

- **Visual Style**: Color grading allows developers to define a specific visual style or mood for their games or scenes, enhancing the overall aesthetic.

- **Color Consistency**: Color correction ensures that colors are accurately represented across different lighting conditions and display devices, providing a consistent visual experience.

- **Cinematic Quality**: Both color grading and correction are used in film production and high-quality games to achieve cinematic quality and realism.

- **Artistic Expression**: These techniques enable artistic expression and creativity, allowing developers to convey emotions and storytelling through colors.

In summary, color grading and correction are powerful tools in computer graphics for achieving specific visual styles, ensuring color accuracy, and enhancing the overall quality and impact of rendered scenes.

4.5 Screen Space Reflections

In this section, we'll explore the concept of Screen Space Reflections (SSR), a post-processing technique used in computer graphics to simulate realistic reflections on surfaces. SSR plays a vital role in enhancing the visual quality and realism of rendered scenes, particularly in environments with reflective materials and dynamic lighting.

Understanding Screen Space Reflections

Screen Space Reflections aim to simulate the reflection of objects and surfaces in a scene based on what is visible on the screen. Unlike traditional reflection mapping techniques that require precomputed reflection maps, SSR operates in screen space, making it suitable for dynamic and complex scenes.

The key idea behind SSR is to trace rays from the camera viewpoint to approximate reflection directions, and then sample the scene to determine what is reflected in each pixel. The reflections are then blended with the scene's colors to create the illusion of reflective surfaces.

Implementation of Screen Space Reflections

Implementing SSR in a post-processing shader involves several steps:

1. **Ray Tracing**: For each pixel on the screen, trace reflection rays in the direction opposite to the camera's view vector. The number of rays and their directions depend on the level of detail required.
2. **Intersection Testing**: For each reflection ray, determine where it intersects with the scene geometry. This involves checking for collisions with objects and surfaces.
3. **Reflection Sampling**: Sample the scene at the intersection point to determine what should be reflected. This includes the colors and materials of nearby surfaces.
4. **Blending**: Blend the reflections with the scene's colors, taking into account factors such as the material's reflectivity and the angle of incidence.

Here's a simplified example of how to implement SSR in a fragment shader:

```glsl
#version 330 core

in vec2 texCoord; // Texture coordinates from the vertex shader

out vec4 fragColor; // Final fragment color

uniform sampler2D colorTexture; // Input rendered image
```

```glsl
uniform sampler2D depthTexture; // Depth buffer

uniform mat4 inverseProjectionMatrix; // Inverse projection matrix

uniform mat4 inverseViewMatrix; // Inverse view matrix

uniform float maxDistance; // Maximum reflection distance

void main() {

// Sample the depth value of the current fragment

float depth = texture(depthTexture, texCoord).r;

// Calculate the world-space position of the fragment

vec4 clipPosition = vec4(texCoord * 2.0 - 1.0, depth * 2.0 - 1.0, 1.0);

vec4 worldPosition = inverseProjectionMatrix * clipPosition;

worldPosition /= worldPosition.w;

// Calculate the reflection ray direction

vec3 viewDirection = normalize(worldPosition.xyz - vec3(inverseViewMatrix[3]));

vec3 reflectionDirection = reflect(viewDirection, vec3(0.0, 0.0, 1.0));

// Trace the reflection ray

vec3 reflectionPosition = worldPosition.xyz;

for (int i = 0; i < NUM_RAY_STEPS; ++i) {

reflectionPosition += reflectionDirection * RAY_STEP_SIZE;

if (reflectionPosition.z > maxDistance) {
```

```
break;

}
```

// *Sample the scene at the reflection position and blend with the color*

// *You would also perform intersection testing here*

```
vec3        reflectedColor        =        texture(colorTexture,
reflectionPosition.xy).rgb;

fragColor.rgb        +=        reflectedColor        *
REFLECTION_BLEND_FACTOR;

}
```

// *Output the final color with reflections*

```
fragColor.a = 1.0;

}
```

In this shader, we sample the depth value of the current fragment to calculate the world-space position. We then determine the reflection ray direction, trace the ray, and sample the scene at each step to blend the reflections with the scene's colors.

Configuring Screen Space Reflections

Configuring SSR involves adjusting parameters such as the maximum reflection distance, the number of reflection rays, and the blending factor. These parameters allow developers to control the level of detail and accuracy of the reflections based on performance and visual quality requirements.

Screen Space Reflections are a valuable post-processing technique in computer graphics, enhancing the realism and visual quality of scenes with reflective surfaces. They are commonly used in games, architectural visualization, and film production to achieve convincing and immersive environments.

Chapter 5: Lighting Mastery

5.1 Global Illumination Techniques

In this section, we will explore the concept of global illumination (GI) techniques in computer graphics. Global illumination is a crucial aspect of rendering realistic and visually appealing scenes by simulating the complex interactions of light in the environment. We will delve into the fundamentals of GI and various techniques used to achieve global illumination effects.

Understanding Global Illumination

Global illumination refers to the process of simulating the indirect lighting in a scene, which includes effects such as diffuse inter-reflection, color bleeding, and soft shadows. Unlike direct lighting, which comes directly from light sources, indirect lighting is a result of light bouncing off surfaces and illuminating other surfaces. Achieving realistic global illumination is challenging because it requires tracing and simulating the paths of light rays as they interact with the scene.

Importance of Global Illumination

Global illumination is essential for several reasons:

1. **Realism**: It enhances the realism of scenes by accurately simulating how light interacts with the environment. This results in more natural-looking lighting and shading.
2. **Ambience**: GI contributes to the overall ambience and mood of a scene by softening shadows, adding color bleeding, and creating a sense of depth.
3. **Visual Quality**: Scenes with global illumination often have

higher visual quality, making them more engaging and immersive for viewers.

Techniques for Global Illumination

Several techniques are used to achieve global illumination in computer graphics. Some of the common approaches include:

- **Radiosity**: Radiosity is a method that simulates the flow of light between surfaces in a scene. It calculates the indirect illumination by solving a system of equations based on the scene's geometry and material properties.

- **Ray Tracing**: Ray tracing is a popular technique for global illumination. It simulates light rays as they travel through the scene, bouncing off surfaces and calculating the cumulative effects of indirect lighting.

- **Photon Mapping**: Photon mapping is a two-step process involving photon emission and photon gathering. It's particularly effective for simulating caustics and complex indirect lighting.

- **Voxel Cone Tracing**: Voxel cone tracing is an optimization technique that involves voxelizing the scene and tracing cones of rays through the voxels to calculate indirect lighting efficiently.

- **Path Tracing**: Path tracing is a Monte Carlo method that simulates the paths of light rays in the scene. It's known for its ability to produce highly realistic global illumination but can be computationally intensive.

Implementing Global Illumination

Implementing global illumination techniques often requires specialized algorithms and considerable computational resources. These techniques can be computationally expensive, and real-time applications like games may use simplified or hybrid methods to approximate global illumination.

Here's a simplified example of how to implement basic global illumination using ray tracing in a fragment shader:

```glsl
#version 330 core

in vec2 texCoord; // Texture coordinates from the vertex shader

out vec4 fragColor; // Final fragment color

uniform sampler2D colorTexture; // Input rendered image

void main() {

// Sample the color from the input image

vec4 directLighting = texture(colorTexture, texCoord);

// Perform additional ray tracing and global illumination calculations here

// Combine direct and indirect lighting

vec3 indirectLighting = /* Compute indirect lighting */;

vec3 finalColor = directLighting.rgb + indirectLighting;

// Output the final color with global illumination

fragColor = vec4(finalColor, 1.0);
```

}

In this simplified shader, we sample the direct lighting from the rendered image and calculate indirect lighting using ray tracing techniques. The final color is obtained by combining direct and indirect lighting.

Significance of Global Illumination

Global illumination is a fundamental concept in computer graphics that significantly impacts the visual quality and realism of rendered scenes. It is widely used in fields such as architectural visualization, film production, and high-quality video games to achieve lifelike lighting and shading effects. Mastery of global illumination techniques is essential for creating visually stunning and immersive digital environments.

5.2 Screen Space Ambient Occlusion (SSAO)

In this section, we will explore the concept of Screen Space Ambient Occlusion (SSAO), a shading technique used in computer graphics to enhance the realism of rendered scenes by simulating the occlusion of ambient light. SSAO is an important component of global illumination and contributes to the overall visual quality of a scene.

Understanding Screen Space Ambient Occlusion

Ambient occlusion is a shading technique that simulates the soft shadows and darkening of areas that are occluded or blocked from receiving direct light. It adds depth and realism to scenes by providing subtle shading effects in crevices, corners, and areas where objects are close to each other.

Screen Space Ambient Occlusion specifically calculates ambient occlusion effects based on the visible information in the screen space. It doesn't require a complete scene representation or a global illumination solution, making it suitable for real-time applications.

Implementation of SSAO

Implementing SSAO involves several steps:

1. **G-buffer**: First, you typically render a G-buffer, which stores information about the scene, including depth, normals, and material properties.
2. **SSAO Pass**: In a separate pass, you calculate ambient occlusion for each pixel in screen space. This is done by sampling neighboring pixels in the G-buffer and comparing their depth values to the current pixel's depth.
3. **Blur Pass**: To achieve a smoother and more subtle effect, you may apply a blur pass to the SSAO result. This helps reduce noise and artifacts.
4. **Combine Pass**: Finally, you combine the SSAO result with the direct and indirect lighting of the scene to obtain the final image.

Here's a simplified example of how to implement SSAO in a fragment shader:

```glsl
#version 330 core

in vec2 texCoord; // Texture coordinates from the vertex shader

out vec4 fragColor; // Final fragment color

uniform sampler2D positionTexture; // G-buffer: position

uniform sampler2D normalTexture; // G-buffer: normal
```

```glsl
uniform sampler2D randomTexture; // Random texture for sampling

uniform float ssaoRadius; // SSAO sampling radius

uniform float ssaoBias; // SSAO depth bias

uniform int ssaoSampleCount; // Number of SSAO samples

void main() {

// Sample the position and normal from the G-buffer

vec3 position = texture(positionTexture, texCoord).xyz;

vec3 normal = texture(normalTexture, texCoord).xyz;

// Initialize the ambient occlusion factor

float ambientOcclusion = 0.0;

// Sample random directions and accumulate ambient occlusion

for (int i = 0; i < ssaoSampleCount; ++i) {

// Sample random direction in hemisphere

vec3 sampleDirection = texture(randomTexture, texCoord * float(i
+ 1)).xyz * 2.0 - 1.0;

// Calculate sample position in view space

vec3 samplePosition = position + sampleDirection * ssaoRadius;

// Transform sample position to screen space

vec4 projectedPosition = projectionMatrix * viewMatrix *
vec4(samplePosition, 1.0);
```

```glsl
vec2 sampleTexCoord = (projectedPosition.xy / projectedPosition.w) * 0.5 + 0.5;

// Calculate occlusion factor based on depth comparison

float sampleDepth = texture(positionTexture, sampleTexCoord).z;

ambientOcclusion += (samplePosition.z - sampleDepth) < ssaoBias ? 1.0 : 0.0;

}

// Calculate final ambient occlusion factor

ambientOcclusion = 1.0 - (ambientOcclusion / float(ssaoSampleCount));

// Output the final color with SSAO

fragColor = vec4(vec3(ambientOcclusion), 1.0);

}
```

In this shader, we sample the position and normal from the G-buffer, then sample random directions and accumulate the ambient occlusion factor based on depth comparisons.

Configuring SSAO

Configuring SSAO involves adjusting parameters such as the sampling radius, depth bias, and the number of SSAO samples. These parameters allow developers to control the strength and visual impact of the ambient occlusion effect.

Screen Space Ambient Occlusion is a valuable post-processing technique in computer graphics that enhances the realism and depth of rendered scenes. It is commonly used in video games, architectural visualization, and film production to improve visual quality and create immersive environments.

5.3 Real-Time Shadow Techniques

In this section, we will explore real-time shadow techniques, a fundamental aspect of computer graphics that adds depth, realism, and immersion to rendered scenes. Shadows play a critical role in creating the perception of three-dimensional objects in a scene and are essential for achieving convincing lighting effects.

Importance of Shadows

Shadows are crucial for several reasons:

1. **Depth and Shape**: Shadows provide visual cues about the depth and shape of objects in a scene. They help viewers perceive the relative positions of objects and their interactions with light.
2. **Realism**: Shadows add realism to scenes by simulating how light interacts with objects. Without shadows, scenes can appear flat and lacking in depth.
3. **Mood and Atmosphere**: Shadows can contribute to the mood and atmosphere of a scene. They can create dramatic or serene effects, depending on the lighting and shadowing choices.
4. **Gameplay and Navigation**: In video games, shadows can have gameplay implications. Players often use shadows for navigation or as cover in stealth games.

Types of Shadows

There are several types of shadows commonly used in real-time computer graphics:

- **Hard Shadows**: Hard shadows have well-defined, sharp edges and are typically produced by a point light source or a directional light source. They are ideal for simulating sunlight or focused light sources.

- **Soft Shadows**: Soft shadows have soft, blurry edges and occur when light scatters or diffuses around an object. Soft shadows are often produced by area light sources or by simulating the finite size of a light source.

- **Dynamic Shadows**: Dynamic shadows are real-time shadows that change as objects and lights move in a scene. These shadows are essential for interactive and dynamic environments, such as video games.

- **Static Shadows**: Static shadows are precomputed or baked shadows that do not change during runtime. They are commonly used in architectural visualization and can be combined with dynamic shadows for added realism.

Shadow Mapping

Shadow mapping is one of the most commonly used techniques for real-time shadow rendering. It involves rendering the scene from the perspective of a light source and storing depth information in a texture called a shadow map. Then, during the final rendering pass, shadow map comparisons are made to determine whether a pixel is in shadow or not.

Here's a simplified example of how to implement basic shadow mapping in a vertex and fragment shader:

Vertex Shader:

#version 330 core

```glsl
layout(location = 0) in vec3 inPosition;

layout(location = 1) in vec2 inTexCoord;

// ... other vertex attributes

uniform mat4 modelMatrix;

uniform mat4 viewMatrix;

uniform mat4 projectionMatrix;

uniform mat4 lightViewMatrix;

uniform mat4 lightProjectionMatrix;

out vec4 fragPosition;

out vec4 lightSpacePosition;

void main() {

// Calculate the world-space position of the vertex

vec4 worldPosition = modelMatrix * vec4(inPosition, 1.0);

// Transform vertex position to light space

lightSpacePosition = lightProjectionMatrix * lightViewMatrix * worldPosition;

// ... other vertex shader code

gl_Position = projectionMatrix * viewMatrix * worldPosition;

}
```

Fragment Shader:

```glsl
#version 330 core
```

```glsl
in vec4 fragPosition;

in vec4 lightSpacePosition;

// ... other interpolated fragment data

uniform sampler2D shadowMap;

uniform float shadowBias;

void main() {

// Project the fragment's position into normalized device coordinates

vec3 fragNDC = fragPosition.xyz / fragPosition.w;

// Transform the fragment's position into the [0,1] range

vec3 shadowMapCoords = 0.5 * lightSpacePosition.xyz + 0.5;

// Compare the depth value from the shadow map with the fragment's depth

float shadow = texture(shadowMap, shadowMapCoords.xy).r;

float visibility = shadowMapCoords.z - shadowBias > shadow ? 1.0 : 0.0;

// ... lighting calculations and other fragment shader code

gl_FragColor = vec4(finalColor * visibility, 1.0);

}
```

In this shadow mapping example, we transform the vertex positions into light space in the vertex shader and perform depth comparisons in the fragment shader to determine whether a fragment is in shadow.

Challenges and Techniques

Implementing real-time shadows can be challenging due to issues such as aliasing, shadow acne, and light bleeding. Various techniques, including percentage-closer filtering (PCF), cascaded shadow maps, and variance shadow mapping, have been developed to address these challenges and improve the quality of real-time shadows.

Real-time shadow rendering is an active area of research and development in computer graphics, and advancements continue to be made to achieve even more realistic and efficient shadow effects in interactive applications.

5.4 Light Probes and Baked Lighting

In this section, we will explore light probes and baked lighting techniques, which are essential tools for achieving realistic lighting in computer graphics. These techniques are commonly used in various applications, including video games, architectural visualization, and film production, to enhance the visual quality and realism of rendered scenes.

Light Probes

Light probes, also known as light probes or environment probes, are objects or data structures used to capture and store information about the surrounding lighting environment. They are particularly useful for simulating indirect lighting and reflections in real-time and offline rendering. Light probes come in various forms:

- **Spherical Harmonics**: Spherical harmonics are a mathematical representation of lighting that captures the color and intensity of light in all directions around a point in space. Spherical harmonics are often used for real-time dynamic lighting and reflections.

• **Cube Maps**: Cube maps are a popular choice for capturing the six faces of a cube, each representing a different direction in space. They are commonly used for environment mapping, skyboxes, and reflections.

• **Light Fields**: Light fields store lighting information for each point in a 3D volume, allowing for dynamic and accurate lighting and reflections.

Light probes are typically placed strategically within a scene to capture the surrounding lighting conditions. They can be used to provide indirect lighting information to objects and characters, improving the overall realism of the scene.

Baked Lighting

Baked lighting, also known as precomputed lighting, is a technique where lighting information is calculated and stored in advance, rather than being computed in real-time. This technique is suitable for scenarios where real-time lighting calculations are too expensive or where the lighting is static or changes infrequently.

The process of baked lighting involves the following steps:

1. **Lighting Calculation**: Lighting is calculated for the scene, often using global illumination techniques like radiosity or ray tracing. The result is typically stored as textures or vertex colors.
2. **Texture Mapping**: The calculated lighting information is mapped onto the scene's surfaces. This can include diffuse and specular lighting, shadows, and ambient occlusion.

3. **Storage**: The computed lighting data is stored in textures or other suitable formats. These textures are then applied to the scene's geometry during rendering.
4. **Rendering**: During real-time rendering, the precomputed lighting data is sampled and used to shade objects in the scene. This can include both direct and indirect lighting effects.

Baked lighting is commonly used in architectural visualization, where lighting conditions are typically static, and real-time rendering performance is crucial. It is also used in video games to improve performance and achieve high-quality lighting in scenes with limited computational resources.

Challenges and Considerations

While light probes and baked lighting offer significant advantages in terms of realism and performance, they come with challenges and considerations:

- **Dynamic Objects**: Baked lighting techniques are less suitable for scenes with dynamic objects or characters that move frequently, as the precomputed lighting data may not adapt to changes.

- **Storage Requirements**: Precomputed lighting data can be storage-intensive, particularly for large and complex scenes. Efficient compression and streaming techniques may be necessary.

- **Artistic Control**: Artists and designers need to carefully set up and adjust baked lighting parameters to achieve the desired visual quality and mood.

- **Hybrid Approaches**: Many real-time applications use hybrid approaches, combining real-time dynamic lighting with precomputed baked lighting for a balance of quality and performance.

Light probes and baked lighting techniques are valuable tools in the field of computer graphics, offering a way to achieve realistic lighting and reflections in interactive applications. Their usage is widespread in a variety of industries, and advancements continue to be made to improve their accuracy and efficiency.

5.5 Volumetric and Subsurface Scattering

In this section, we will explore the concepts of volumetric rendering and subsurface scattering (SSS), both of which are essential for achieving realistic lighting and materials in computer graphics. Volumetric rendering allows for the representation of participating media, such as fog, smoke, and clouds, while subsurface scattering is responsible for the realistic appearance of translucent and semi-transparent materials like skin, wax, and certain types of fruit.

Volumetric Rendering

Volumetric rendering involves simulating the interaction of light with participating media within a 3D space. This technique is used to create effects such as fog, smoke, dust, and atmospheric scattering. Volumetric rendering is crucial for adding depth and realism to scenes, especially in outdoor environments and when portraying natural phenomena.

Techniques for Volumetric Rendering

Several techniques are used for volumetric rendering:

- **Ray Marching**: This technique involves tracing rays through a volume, stepping along each ray and accumulating color and opacity as it interacts with the media.

- **Volume Textures**: Volumetric data can be stored in 3D textures, allowing for efficient sampling and rendering. This is common in scientific visualization and medical imaging.

- **Particle Systems**: In some cases, individual particles are used to represent the volume, and their interactions with light are simulated individually or in groups.

- **Screen-Space Effects**: Some real-time applications use screen-space effects to simulate volumetric effects quickly and efficiently.

Volumetric rendering techniques can be computationally expensive, especially when dealing with complex scenes or high-resolution volumes. Optimization and approximations are often used to balance quality and performance.

Subsurface Scattering (SSS)

Subsurface scattering is a rendering technique used to simulate the behavior of light as it penetrates and scatters within translucent or semi-transparent materials. It is essential for achieving the realistic appearance of materials such as skin, wax, marble, and some types of fruits. SSS is particularly noticeable in areas where light enters the material and then exits at a different location.

Techniques for Subsurface Scattering

Implementing subsurface scattering typically involves the following steps:

1. **Material Properties**: Define material properties that describe how light scatters within the material. This includes parameters like diffusion and absorption coefficients.
2. **Light Transport**: Calculate how light enters the material, scatters within it, and exits. This can be done using diffusion theory or more complex methods like Monte Carlo ray tracing.
3. **Multiple Layers**: Some materials have multiple layers with different scattering properties, requiring more complex models.
4. **Rendering**: Apply the subsurface scattering model during rendering, often as a post-processing effect.

Here's a simplified example of how to simulate subsurface scattering in a fragment shader:

```glsl
#version 330 core

in vec2 texCoord; // Texture coordinates from the vertex shader

out vec4 fragColor; // Final fragment color

uniform sampler2D colorTexture; // Input texture

uniform sampler2D normalTexture; // Normal map

uniform float scatteringCoefficient; // Scattering coefficient

void main() {
```

```
// Sample the color and normal from the textures

vec3 color = texture(colorTexture, texCoord).rgb;

vec3 normal = normalize(texture(normalTexture, texCoord).xyz);

// Calculate the subsurface scattering effect

vec3 subsurfaceColor = color * scatteringCoefficient;

// Combine the original color and subsurface scattering color

vec3 finalColor = color + subsurfaceColor;

// Output the final color with subsurface scattering

fragColor = vec4(finalColor, 1.0);

}
```

In this simplified shader, we sample the color and normal from textures and add subsurface scattering by multiplying the color with a scattering coefficient.

Significance of Volumetric Rendering and SSS

Volumetric rendering and subsurface scattering are essential techniques in computer graphics for achieving realistic and visually engaging scenes. They are widely used in industries such as film, animation, gaming, and architectural visualization to create lifelike materials and environments. Their successful implementation requires a balance between computational complexity and visual fidelity, making them active areas of research and development in the field of computer graphics.

Chapter 6: Advanced Camera Techniques

6.1 Cinematic Camera Effects

In this section, we will delve into the world of cinematic camera effects used in computer graphics and game development. Cinematic camera techniques are essential for creating visually engaging and immersive experiences, whether in movies, video games, or virtual reality applications. These effects go beyond the standard camera controls and allow developers and filmmakers to evoke emotions, emphasize storytelling, and enhance the overall visual quality of the project.

Depth of Field (DOF)

Depth of field is a fundamental cinematic effect that simulates the focus characteristics of real-world cameras. It controls which objects in the scene appear sharp and in focus while blurring objects at other depths. This effect can be used to draw the viewer's attention to a specific subject or create a sense of depth and realism.

In computer graphics, depth of field is typically achieved using one of two main methods:

1. **Post-processing**: Post-processing depth of field is applied as a shader effect during the rendering process. It involves calculating the depth of each pixel in the scene and then applying a blur based on the distance from the camera focal point. Here's a simplified example of a depth of field shader in GLSL:

```
// Sample the depth buffer to get the depth of the current pixel

float depth = texture(depthTexture, texCoord).r;

// Calculate the depth of field based on the depth and focal length

float focalDepth = /* focal depth value */;

float blurAmount = abs(depth - focalDepth) * /* blur scale factor */;

// Apply the blur effect to the pixel color

vec3 blurredColor = texture(colorTexture, texCoord + blurAmount * /* blur direction */).rgb;

// Output the final color

fragColor = vec4(blurredColor, 1.0);
```

1. **Lens Simulation**: A more physically accurate approach involves simulating the camera lens characteristics, including the lens aperture, focal length, and lens imperfections. This method requires ray tracing or other advanced rendering techniques to accurately model how light rays pass through the camera lens.

Depth of field is not only about blurring objects but also about controlling the aperture size to determine how much light enters the camera. A wide aperture (small f-number) results in a shallow depth of field, while a narrow aperture (large f-number) increases the depth of field.

Motion Blur

Motion blur is another cinematic effect that simulates the way objects and the camera capture motion in the real world. When an object or camera moves rapidly, a motion blur effect occurs, where the object appears streaked or blurred along its path of motion. Motion blur helps convey a sense of speed and realism in dynamic scenes.

There are two primary methods to implement motion blur in computer graphics:

1. **Object Motion Blur**: This technique applies motion blur separately to individual objects in the scene. It involves rendering multiple positions of each moving object over time and blending them together. The degree of blur depends on the object's velocity and the duration of the exposure.

2. **Camera Motion Blur**: Camera motion blur simulates the motion of the entire camera. It involves tracking the camera's position and orientation over time and then rendering the scene multiple times from slightly different viewpoints. The resulting frames are then blended to create the motion blur effect.

Implementing motion blur requires careful consideration of factors such as shutter speed, object velocities, and the number of motion blur samples. Additionally, motion blur can be computationally expensive, so optimization techniques may be necessary for real-time applications.

These cinematic camera effects, including depth of field and motion blur, play a crucial role in creating visually captivating and immersive experiences in computer graphics and game development. When used effectively, they can significantly enhance storytelling and audience engagement.

6.2 Camera Paths and Splines

In this section, we will explore camera paths and splines, which are essential techniques for controlling the movement and animation of cameras in computer graphics and game development. Camera paths and splines provide a means to create smooth and dynamic camera movements, enabling developers to craft visually appealing scenes and gameplay experiences.

Understanding Camera Paths

A camera path is a predefined trajectory or route that a camera follows within a 3D environment. It specifies the camera's position and orientation at each point along the path, allowing for precise control over camera movement. Camera paths are particularly useful for creating cinematic sequences, cutscenes, and scripted events in games and animations.

Linear Paths

The simplest form of a camera path is a linear path, where the camera moves in a straight line from one point to another. Linear paths are easy to implement and provide straightforward movement. However, they may not always produce the most visually engaging results, especially for cinematic sequences.

Here's a basic example of linear camera interpolation in pseudocode:

```
def linear_interpolation(start_point, end_point, t):
    # t is a value between 0 and 1 representing the progress along the path
```

t = clamp(t, 0, 1)

return start_point + (end_point - start_point) * t

Bezier Splines

Bezier splines are a more advanced and versatile method for defining camera paths. A Bezier spline uses control points to shape the curve along which the camera moves. This allows for smooth and curved paths, which can create more visually pleasing and natural camera movements.

There are several types of Bezier splines, including:

- **Linear Bezier**: Uses two control points to create a linear segment.

- **Quadratic Bezier**: Uses three control points for quadratic curves.

- **Cubic Bezier**: Uses four control points for cubic curves.

Here's a simplified example of a cubic Bezier interpolation in pseudocode:

def cubic_bezier_interpolation(p0, p1, p2, p3, t):

 # t is a value between 0 and 1 representing the progress along the path

t = clamp(t, 0, 1)

u = 1 - t

tt = t * t

uu = u * u

uuu = uu * u

ttt = tt * t

p = uuu * p0

p += 3 * uu * t * p1

p += 3 * u * tt * p2

p += ttt * p3

return p

Interpolating Camera Parameters

In addition to interpolating camera positions, camera paths often involve interpolating other parameters such as camera orientation (rotation), field of view (FOV), and focal length. These parameters contribute to the overall cinematic quality of camera movements.

Creating Camera Animations

To create camera animations using camera paths and splines, developers typically define keyframes that specify the camera's state at specific points in time. These keyframes are then interpolated to generate a smooth animation. Additionally, easing functions can be applied to control the acceleration and deceleration of the camera's movement, creating more cinematic transitions between keyframes.

In practice, camera path and spline systems are often integrated into game engines and animation software, simplifying the process of creating camera animations. These systems provide tools for defining paths, keyframes, and easing functions, allowing developers and animators to focus on crafting compelling camera sequences.

Overall, camera paths and splines are powerful tools for adding dynamic and visually appealing camera animations to games, simulations, and animations. They enable creators to tell stories and guide player experiences with precision and artistry.

6.3 First-Person and Third-Person Camera Systems

In this section, we will explore two common camera systems used in computer games and simulations: first-person and third-person camera systems. These camera perspectives significantly influence the player's experience and interaction with the virtual environment.

First-Person Camera

The first-person camera, often referred to as the "FPS" or "first-person shooter" camera, provides a view from the protagonist's perspective. In this camera mode, players perceive the game world as if they are looking through the eyes of the in-game character. The first-person perspective creates a strong sense of immersion, as it closely resembles human vision.

Key Characteristics of First-Person Cameras:

1. **Field of View (FOV):** The FOV in a first-person camera system is typically set to mimic human vision, usually around 90 to 120 degrees. This FOV provides a natural and immersive view of the game world.
2. **Head Movement:** First-person cameras often simulate subtle head movements as players look around, adding to the feeling of presence within the game.
3. **Weapon and Hand Models:** To enhance immersion, first-person games often include 3D models of the character's

hands and held weapons or items. These models move and animate in response to player actions.

4. **Mouse or Controller Input**: Players control the direction of their view using a mouse or thumbsticks on a game controller. This input method allows for precise aiming and looking.

5. **Crosshair**: A crosshair or reticle is often displayed at the center of the screen to aid in targeting and aiming.

Third-Person Camera

The third-person camera provides a view of the game world from a position behind and slightly above the player character. This perspective offers a broader view of the character and their surroundings, making it easier to navigate and interact with the environment.

Key Characteristics of Third-Person Cameras:

1. **Over-the-Shoulder or Fixed**: Third-person cameras can be designed as over-the-shoulder cameras, where the camera is positioned just behind and to the side of the character, or as fixed cameras that maintain a consistent distance and angle from the character.

2. **Character Visibility**: In third-person games, the player character is often visible on the screen. This allows players to see their character's actions, appearance, and animations.

3. **Manual or Automatic Control**: Some third-person games provide players with direct control over the camera, allowing them to adjust the camera angle as needed. In other cases, the camera is automatically controlled by the game to maintain an optimal view.

4. **Obstacle Avoidance**: To prevent the camera from

becoming obstructed by objects in the game world, third-person camera systems often include algorithms for obstacle avoidance and camera clipping.

5. **Contextual Views**: Third-person cameras may dynamically adjust their position and angle based on the context of the gameplay, ensuring that important actions and events remain visible.

Choosing the Right Camera System

The choice between a first-person and third-person camera system depends on the type of game, gameplay mechanics, and the desired player experience. First-person cameras excel in games that prioritize immersion and precise aiming, such as first-person shooters and virtual reality experiences. On the other hand, third-person cameras are well-suited for games that emphasize character visibility, exploration, and platforming.

In some cases, games may even offer both camera perspectives, allowing players to switch between them as needed. This flexibility can cater to a broader audience and accommodate different gameplay scenarios within the same game.

Implementing effective first-person and third-person camera systems requires careful consideration of camera controls, character animations, collision detection, and player feedback. When executed well, these camera perspectives can greatly enhance the player's connection to the virtual world and contribute to a satisfying gaming experience.

6.4 Dynamic Camera Effects

In this section, we will explore dynamic camera effects in the context of computer graphics and game development. Dynamic camera effects are techniques that enhance the visual and interactive aspects of a game by modifying the camera's behavior or view in response to gameplay events, user input, or scripted sequences. These effects can be used to create more engaging and immersive gaming experiences.

Dynamic Camera Control

Dynamic camera control involves adjusting the camera's position, orientation, and field of view in real-time to respond to various game events and conditions. Here are some common scenarios where dynamic camera control is applied:

1. Player Character Movement

In many games, the camera follows the player character as they move through the game world. Dynamic camera control ensures that the camera smoothly tracks the character's position and orientation, providing a clear and informative view of the surroundings.

 # Pseudo-code for dynamic camera following the player character

camera_position = lerp(camera_position, player_position, smoothing_factor * delta_time)

camera_look_at = player_position

2. Cinematic Cutscenes

During scripted sequences or cutscenes, the camera can be controlled to create dramatic or cinematic views. This might involve transitioning to specific camera angles, zooming in on characters, or using visual effects such as depth of field or motion blur for added impact.

 # Pseudo-code for cinematic camera transition

if in_cutscene:

camera_position = lerp(camera_position, target_position, transition_speed * delta_time)

camera_look_at = target_position

3. Game Events

In response to in-game events, such as explosions, collisions, or important objectives, the camera can be briefly adjusted to draw the player's attention or provide a dynamic view of the action.

 # Pseudo-code for dynamic camera adjustment during an explosion

if explosion_occurred:

camera_shake_intensity = explosion_intensity

Camera Shakes and Effects

Camera shakes and effects are impactful dynamic camera techniques that simulate environmental or gameplay events that affect the camera's stability. These effects add a level of realism and intensity to the player's experience.

1. Camera Shakes

Camera shakes replicate the feeling of vibrations, tremors, or impact forces. They are commonly used in action games to convey the sensation of powerful explosions, collisions, or heavy impacts. Camera shakes are implemented by perturbing the camera's position and orientation over a short duration.

 # Pseudo-code for camera shake effect

if shake_intensity > 0:

camera_offset = random_vector_in_unit_sphere() * shake_intensity

2. Screen Flash and Post-processing

In response to critical moments, damage, or certain gameplay events, screen flashes, color grading, and other post-processing effects can be applied to the camera's view. These effects alter the visual presentation of the game temporarily to emphasize or communicate specific situations.

 # Pseudo-code for screen flash effect

if player_takes_damage:

flash_duration = damage_flash_duration

User-Controlled Dynamic Effects

Some games empower players to control dynamic camera effects to enhance gameplay. For example, a sniper rifle scope might allow players to zoom in and focus on distant targets, or a detective mode in an investigative game might reveal hidden clues.

 # Pseudo-code for user-controlled camera zoom

if using_sniper_rifle:

camera_field_of_view = sniper_zoom_fov

Implementing Dynamic Camera Effects

The implementation of dynamic camera effects varies widely depending on the game engine and programming language used. Many game engines provide built-in tools and scripting capabilities to facilitate the creation of dynamic camera behaviors. It's essential to strike a balance between using these effects to enhance gameplay and avoiding overuse that could disrupt the player's experience.

Dynamic camera effects play a crucial role in creating immersive and engaging games. When applied thoughtfully and in sync with gameplay, they contribute to a more cinematic and enjoyable gaming experience, enhancing player immersion and emotional engagement with the game world.

6.5 VR Camera Systems and Considerations

In this section, we will delve into virtual reality (VR) camera systems and the unique considerations involved in creating immersive VR experiences. VR is a technology that places users inside a simulated 3D environment, and as a result, the camera systems for VR differ significantly from traditional game cameras.

The Essence of VR

VR aims to replicate the perception of being physically present in a computer-generated world. To achieve this, VR systems employ specialized hardware, such as VR headsets, motion controllers, and tracking sensors. These components work together to provide users with a sense of immersion and presence.

VR Camera Basics

In VR, the concept of a camera is somewhat different from traditional games. Instead of a virtual camera controlled by the player or developer, VR relies on the user's physical head movements and the headset's tracking system to determine the view.

1. Head-Relative Tracking

In VR, the user's head becomes the camera. The VR headset continuously tracks the user's head position and orientation in real-time, allowing the user to look around and interact with the virtual world naturally.

 # Pseudo-code for updating the VR camera based on head tracking

headset_position = get_headset_position()

headset_rotation = get_headset_rotation()

2. Stereoscopic Rendering

VR systems utilize stereoscopic rendering to create depth perception. Two slightly different images are rendered for each eye, mimicking the way human vision works. These images are then presented to the user's eyes through the VR headset's lenses, creating a 3D effect.

 # Pseudo-code for rendering separate views for each eye

left_eye_view = render_scene_from_eye(camera_position_left, camera_rotation_left)

right_eye_view = render_scene_from_eye(camera_position_right, camera_rotation_right)

User Interaction

Interactivity is a fundamental aspect of VR experiences. VR games and applications often enable users to interact with the virtual world using motion controllers or other input devices. These interactions can include grabbing objects, pointing, shooting, or using hand gestures.

 # Pseudo-code for handling user interactions in VR

if controller_button_pressed():

interact_with_object()

VR Comfort and Motion Sickness

VR developers must consider user comfort to avoid motion sickness, a common challenge in VR experiences. Motion sickness occurs when there is a disconnect between the user's visual perception and their inner ear's sense of balance. To mitigate this, VR applications often employ techniques like smooth locomotion, comfort vignettes, and teleportation.

 # Pseudo-code for implementing teleportation in VR

if teleport_button_pressed():

move_to_target_location()

Performance Considerations

VR places high demands on hardware performance. VR applications must maintain a high and consistent frame rate to prevent motion sickness and ensure a smooth experience. Optimizing rendering and minimizing latency are critical considerations in VR development.

 # Pseudo-code for measuring and optimizing VR frame rate

if frame_rate_below_threshold():

optimize_rendering_pipeline()

Conclusion

Creating VR camera systems is a unique and exciting challenge in game and application development. VR's ability to immerse users in virtual worlds requires careful attention to user comfort, interaction design, and performance optimization. When executed effectively, VR camera systems can deliver incredibly immersive and memorable experiences that blur the line between reality and the virtual world.

Chapter 7: Particle Systems and Effects

7.1 Particle System Basics

In this section, we will delve into the fundamentals of particle systems in computer graphics and game development. Particle systems are widely used to simulate and render various phenomena such as fire, smoke, sparks, rain, and many other dynamic effects. Understanding particle systems is essential for creating visually compelling and dynamic game worlds.

What Are Particle Systems?

A particle system is a technique used to model and simulate a large number of small, individual objects called particles. These particles can represent various elements, such as water droplets, debris, or even abstract entities like magic spells. By simulating the behavior and movement of these particles over time, we can create dynamic and visually appealing effects.

Key Components of a Particle System:

1. **Particles**: The basic building blocks of a particle system are the individual particles. Each particle has properties such as position, velocity, size, color, and lifespan.
2. **Emitter**: The emitter is the source from which particles are spawned. It defines the initial properties of the particles, such as their position, velocity, and emission rate.
3. **Behavior Rules**: Particle systems are governed by a set of rules that define how particles evolve over time. These rules can include physics simulations, forces, and constraints.
4. **Renderer**: The renderer is responsible for visualizing the

particles on the screen. It determines how particles are drawn, textured, lit, and blended with the background.

Particle System Workflow

The creation and simulation of a particle system typically follow these steps:

1. **Initialization**: Define the emitter properties, such as the initial position, velocity, and emission rate. Set up the behavior rules and parameters.
2. **Particle Spawning**: Continuously spawn new particles from the emitter based on the defined emission rate and initial properties.
3. **Update**: In each frame of the simulation, update the properties of all existing particles based on the behavior rules. This includes updating positions, velocities, sizes, colors, and lifespans.
4. **Simulation**: Apply physics simulations, forces, and constraints to achieve the desired particle behavior. For example, gravity can affect particles' trajectories, wind can push them, and collision detection can make them bounce.
5. **Rendering**: Render the particles to the screen using the specified rendering techniques. This can involve point sprites, billboards, or custom shaders for various effects.
6. **Particle Removal**: Remove particles that have exceeded their lifespan or are no longer visible to optimize performance and memory usage.

Common Uses of Particle Systems

Particle systems are versatile and find applications in various aspects of game development, including:

- **Visual Effects**: Creating realistic or stylized effects like fire, smoke, explosions, and magic spells.

- **Environmental Effects**: Simulating natural phenomena such as rain, snow, leaves falling, or underwater bubbles.

- **Gameplay Feedback**: Providing feedback to players through visual cues like hit sparks, damage indicators, or power-up effects.

- **Ambiance and Atmosphere**: Enhancing the atmosphere of the game world with effects like fog, mist, or falling leaves.

- **User Interface**: Creating interactive and animated elements in the user interface, such as menu transitions, loading screens, and HUD elements.

Performance Considerations

Efficiently handling a large number of particles can be computationally intensive. Game developers need to optimize their particle systems to maintain a smooth frame rate. This can involve techniques like particle pooling, level-of-detail (LOD) for distant particles, and GPU acceleration.

In the next sections, we will dive deeper into specific aspects of particle systems, including GPU-accelerated particles, smoke and fire simulations, water and fluid dynamics, and cloth and soft body dynamics, expanding your knowledge of these essential visual effects in game development.

7.2 GPU-Accelerated Particles

In this section, we'll explore the concept of GPU-accelerated particles, a technique used to improve the performance and visual fidelity of particle systems in real-time applications, particularly games. GPU acceleration leverages the power of modern graphics hardware to handle large numbers of particles efficiently, allowing for more complex and visually appealing effects.

The Need for GPU Acceleration

Traditional CPU-based particle systems are limited in the number of particles they can simulate in real-time due to the CPU's processing capacity. As game environments have become more complex and demanding, the desire for more particles and richer effects has grown. GPU acceleration addresses this need by offloading particle calculations to the graphics processing unit (GPU), which excels at parallel processing.

How GPU-Accelerated Particles Work

GPU-accelerated particle systems follow a similar workflow to CPU-based systems but with a key difference. Instead of relying solely on the CPU to update particle properties, GPU-accelerated systems perform particle calculations directly on the GPU, taking advantage of its massively parallel architecture.

Key Components of GPU-Accelerated Particles:

1. **Particle Data Buffer**: Particle properties such as position, velocity, size, and color are stored in a GPU buffer, which can be efficiently read and modified by the GPU.
2. **Compute Shaders**: Compute shaders are GPU programs designed for parallel processing tasks. In the context of

particle systems, compute shaders perform calculations on particle data in parallel. These calculations can include position updates, physics simulations, and collision detection.

3. **Render Shaders**: Render shaders are responsible for rendering particles on the screen. They take the updated particle data from the compute shaders and generate the visual representation of particles, often using techniques like billboarding or point sprites.

Advantages of GPU-Accelerated Particles

1. **High Particle Counts**: GPU acceleration allows for the simulation and rendering of a significantly higher number of particles than CPU-based systems. This is especially valuable for effects like dense smoke, swarming insects, or large-scale explosions.
2. **Parallel Processing**: GPUs excel at parallel processing, enabling efficient simulations of particle behaviors across thousands or even millions of particles simultaneously.
3. **Realism and Complexity**: With more particles at your disposal, you can create visually complex and realistic effects. Particles can interact with each other, respond to environmental forces, and exhibit complex behaviors.
4. **Improved Performance**: By offloading particle calculations to the GPU, you free up CPU resources for other game logic, resulting in improved overall performance.

GPU-Accelerated Particle Challenges

While GPU-accelerated particles offer significant benefits, they also present challenges:

1. **Development Complexity**: Implementing GPU-accelerated particle systems can be more complex than CPU-based systems, as it involves writing and debugging compute shaders.
2. **Memory Management**: Efficiently managing GPU memory for particle data is crucial. Developers must avoid memory leaks and ensure data is transferred between the CPU and GPU efficiently.
3. **Platform Compatibility**: Compatibility with different graphics hardware and APIs (e.g., DirectX, Vulkan, OpenGL) can be a concern. Developers may need to optimize shaders for different platforms.
4. **Synchronization**: Synchronizing data between the CPU and GPU can introduce overhead. Strategies like double buffering or asynchronous data transfer can help mitigate this.
5. **Debugging Challenges**: Debugging GPU-accelerated particle systems can be more challenging than debugging CPU-based systems. Tools and techniques for GPU debugging are essential.

Despite these challenges, the performance gains and visual quality improvements offered by GPU-accelerated particles make them a valuable tool for game developers looking to create immersive and visually stunning effects in their games and applications.

7.3 Smoke and Fire Simulations

In this section, we will explore the simulation and rendering of smoke and fire, two common and visually captivating effects in game development. These effects play a crucial role in enhancing realism and immersing players in virtual worlds. Achieving convincing smoke and fire simulations involves a combination of physics, particle systems, and rendering techniques.

Understanding Smoke and Fire

Smoke: Smoke is composed of tiny particles or aerosols suspended in the air. It typically appears as a diffuse, semi-transparent cloud and is often generated by processes like combustion, heating, or explosions.

Fire: Fire is the visible result of the combustion process. It emits light and heat and is characterized by its dynamic, flickering, and swirling appearance. Fire consists of hot gases, flames, and glowing particles.

Particle-Based Simulations

Particle systems are commonly used to simulate both smoke and fire. These systems create the illusion of complex fluid dynamics by emitting and animating a large number of particles that collectively represent the appearance and behavior of the effect.

Smoke Simulation: Simulating smoke involves emitting particles that rise and disperse over time. These particles may be affected by forces like buoyancy, wind, and turbulence, creating the characteristic appearance of smoke plumes.

Fire Simulation: Fire simulations require more complex interactions. In addition to rising particles, fire involves the creation and destruction of particles due to combustion. Heat, light emission, and color changes are also simulated to capture the appearance of flames.

Fluid Dynamics

For more advanced and realistic simulations, fluid dynamics techniques can be applied. Fluid simulations simulate the flow and interactions of gases and liquids, allowing for dynamic behavior that reacts to external forces and influences the surrounding environment.

Smoke and Fire as Fluids: In fluid simulations, smoke and fire are treated as dynamic fluids with properties like density, temperature, and velocity. These simulations can produce highly realistic results but are computationally intensive.

Rendering Techniques

Rendering smoke and fire involves capturing their visual characteristics, including opacity, illumination, and color variations. Various rendering techniques are employed to achieve convincing visual results:

Volume Rendering: Volume rendering techniques treat the smoke or fire simulation as a 3D volume, allowing for realistic light absorption, scattering, and emission within the volume. This approach is computationally intensive but can produce stunning visuals.

Particle Rendering: Particle systems used for simulation can also be used for rendering. Particles are rendered as points or sprites, and techniques like additive blending and motion blur are applied to create the illusion of smoke and fire.

Shader Effects: Custom shaders can be used to enhance the appearance of smoke and fire. Shaders can simulate light emission, color changes, and dynamic effects like turbulence and distortion.

Realism and Optimization

Balancing realism and performance is a critical consideration when implementing smoke and fire simulations. Realistic simulations can be computationally expensive, so optimization techniques are often necessary.

Level of Detail (LOD): LOD techniques can be applied to reduce simulation complexity for distant smoke and fire effects. Distant effects may use simplified simulations to save computational resources.

Culling and Occlusion: Techniques like frustum culling and occlusion culling help prevent unnecessary simulation and rendering of off-screen smoke and fire.

GPU Acceleration: Leveraging the GPU for both simulation and rendering can significantly improve performance, especially for particle-based simulations.

In conclusion, smoke and fire simulations are essential for creating immersive and visually striking game environments. Achieving convincing results requires a combination of particle-based simulations, fluid dynamics, and advanced rendering techniques. Balancing realism and performance is crucial for delivering engaging and responsive gameplay experiences.

7.4 Water and Fluid Dynamics

In this section, we will explore the simulation and rendering of water and fluid dynamics, which are essential for creating realistic and visually engaging environments in games and simulations. Simulating the behavior of water and fluids involves complex physics and mathematical models, but the results can be breathtaking.

Understanding Water and Fluids

Water and fluids in the context of computer graphics refer to substances that flow and interact with their surroundings. Water, in particular, is a critical element in many game environments, from serene lakes and rivers to turbulent oceans and dynamic rain effects. Simulating fluids, on the other hand, extends beyond water and can include liquids, gases, and even abstract substances.

Fluid Simulation Techniques

Simulating the behavior of fluids, including water, typically involves using computational fluid dynamics (CFD) techniques. These techniques solve a set of mathematical equations that describe fluid motion and interactions. There are various approaches to fluid simulation:

Eulerian vs. Lagrangian: Eulerian methods focus on solving equations at fixed points in space, while Lagrangian methods track the motion of individual fluid particles. Eulerian methods are often used for grid-based simulations, while Lagrangian methods are employed in particle-based simulations.

Grid-Based Simulations: Grid-based methods divide space into a grid and solve fluid equations at each grid cell. These methods are suitable for simulating large-scale fluid behavior, such as oceans and rivers. Techniques like the Navier-Stokes equations are commonly used.

Particle-Based Simulations: Particle-based methods simulate fluids by representing them as a collection of particles. Each particle carries properties like position, velocity, and density. Particle systems are well-suited for small-scale fluid behavior like splashes, smoke, and water droplets.

Realistic Water Rendering

Once fluid behavior is simulated, rendering techniques are applied to create visually convincing water surfaces. Realistic water rendering involves several key components:

Surface Waves: Surface waves are essential for creating the appearance of water ripples, waves, and reflections. Techniques like Gerstner waves or FFT-based methods can be used to simulate waves.

Reflections and Refractions: Water reflects and refracts light, creating the illusion of transparency. Real-time rendering techniques like cube maps or screen-space reflections are used to capture these effects.

Caustics: Caustics are the patterns of light refracted through a transparent surface, such as water. Achieving caustics in real-time rendering can be computationally expensive but adds a high level of realism.

Dynamic Ripples and Splashes: Dynamic effects like ripples from raindrops, splashes from objects hitting the water, and foam generation enhance the realism of water surfaces.

Optimization and Performance

Simulating and rendering complex water and fluid dynamics can be computationally demanding. To maintain good performance, developers often employ optimization techniques:

Level of Detail (LOD): Implementing LOD techniques to reduce simulation and rendering complexity for distant bodies of water or less visible fluid effects.

Culling: Utilizing frustum culling and occlusion culling to avoid simulating and rendering water and fluids that are not in the player's view.

GPU Acceleration: Leveraging the GPU for both fluid simulation and rendering to take advantage of its parallel processing capabilities.

In conclusion, water and fluid dynamics play a crucial role in creating realistic and immersive game environments. Simulating fluid behavior requires a solid understanding of fluid dynamics principles, and achieving convincing visuals involves a combination of simulation and rendering techniques. Balancing realism with performance optimization is essential for delivering engaging and responsive gameplay experiences.

7.5 Cloth and Soft Body Dynamics

In this section, we will delve into the simulation and rendering of cloth and soft body dynamics, two essential aspects of game development that contribute to realism and interactivity in virtual worlds. Cloth simulations are commonly used for simulating garments, flags, and flexible materials, while soft body dynamics extend to simulate deformable objects and characters.

Cloth Simulation

Cloth as a Grid: Cloth simulations often start with a grid of particles representing the cloth's vertices. These particles are

connected by constraints that define how they move relative to
each other.

*Physics-Based Cloth Models: Various physics-based models are
used to simulate cloth behavior. The most common model is the
mass-spring-damper system, which treats cloth as a collection of
masses (particles), springs (constraints), and dampers (to control
motion).*

*Forces and Constraints: Forces such as gravity, wind, and external
impacts act on the cloth particles, causing them to move.
Constraints maintain the cloth's shape and prevent it from
collapsing or self-intersecting.*

*Simulation Techniques: Implicit and explicit integration methods
are used to update cloth particle positions over time. Implicit
methods are stable but computationally intensive, while explicit
methods are faster but may require smaller time steps.*

Soft Body Dynamics

*Deformable Objects: Soft body dynamics extend beyond cloth to
simulate the behavior of deformable objects. This can include
characters, creatures, and objects made of soft or elastic materials.*

*Mass-Spring Systems: Similar to cloth, soft body dynamics often
use mass-spring systems to represent deformable objects. These
systems model the object's internal structure with masses
connected by springs.*

*Collision Handling: Handling collisions with other objects and
the environment is crucial for realistic soft body simulations.*

Collision detection and response algorithms ensure that soft bodies interact appropriately with their surroundings.

Realistic Deformation: Soft body simulations aim to capture the realistic deformation of objects under various forces and constraints. This includes stretching, bending, twisting, and compression.

Rendering Cloth and Soft Bodies

Vertex-Based Deformation: Cloth and soft bodies are typically rendered using vertex-based deformation. The positions of vertices are updated based on the simulated deformations.

Skinning: For characters and creatures with soft body parts, skinning techniques are used to bind the soft body to a rigid skeleton. This allows for realistic movement and deformation of character models.

Materials and Shaders: Materials for cloth and soft bodies require shaders that account for their physical properties, such as elasticity, friction, and stretching resistance. These shaders control how light interacts with the surfaces.

Performance Considerations

Optimization: Cloth and soft body simulations can be computationally expensive. Optimization techniques, including spatial partitioning, culling, and parallelization, are employed to maintain real-time performance.

Level of Detail (LOD): LOD techniques are applied to reduce the complexity of simulations and rendering for objects that are distant or less visible.

Hardware Acceleration: Utilizing hardware acceleration, especially on modern GPUs, can significantly improve the performance of cloth and soft body simulations.

In conclusion, cloth and soft body dynamics are essential for creating realistic and interactive game environments. Simulating the behavior of cloth and deformable objects requires a combination of physics-based models, constraint systems, and collision handling. Rendering these simulations involves updating vertex positions and applying appropriate materials and shaders. Balancing realism with performance optimization is crucial for delivering engaging and responsive gameplay experiences.

Chapter 8: Scene Management and Loading

8.1 Scene Graphs and Hierarchies

Scene management and loading are fundamental aspects of game development, as they determine how game worlds are organized, loaded, and rendered. In this section, we will explore the concept of scene graphs and hierarchies, which provide a structured way to manage and represent the elements within a game scene.

Understanding Scene Graphs

A scene graph is a data structure that represents the hierarchy and organization of objects in a game scene. It is a tree-like structure where each node represents an object or a group of objects in the scene. Scene graphs are essential for various purposes, including rendering, physics simulation, and interactions.

Nodes and Transformations: Each node in a scene graph typically stores information about an object's position, orientation, scale, and other transformations. These transformations are applied relative to the node's parent, allowing objects to be positioned and animated within a hierarchy.

Parent-Child Relationships: Nodes in a scene graph form parent-child relationships. Transformations applied to a parent node affect all its child nodes. This hierarchical structure is useful for creating complex scenes with relative positioning and animation.

Object Types: Nodes can represent a wide range of object types, such as 3D models, lights, cameras, particle systems, and more.

Scene graphs allow different types of objects to be organized within the same structure.

Benefits of Scene Graphs

Scene graphs offer several advantages for game development:

Efficient Transformations: By storing transformations at each node, scene graphs allow for efficient computation of object positions and orientations. This is crucial for rendering and physics simulations.

Hierarchical Organization: The hierarchy of scene graphs mirrors the organization of objects in the game world. This makes it easier to work with complex scenes and perform operations on groups of objects.

Culling and Optimization: Scene graphs enable culling techniques like frustum culling and occlusion culling. Objects that are not visible can be skipped during rendering, improving performance.

Animation and Interactivity: Scene graphs are ideal for animating objects and handling interactive behaviors. Animations can be applied to individual nodes or entire branches of the hierarchy.

Implementing Scene Graphs

Traversal Algorithms: Traversal algorithms are used to traverse a scene graph and perform operations on nodes. Depth-first and breadth-first traversal are common approaches. These algorithms are used for rendering, picking, and other scene-related tasks.

Loading and Serialization: Scene graphs can be saved to and loaded from external files, allowing for the creation of complex scenes in content creation tools. Serialization formats like JSON or XML are often used for this purpose.

Dynamic Scene Changes: Scene graphs support dynamic changes to the scene, such as adding or removing objects, updating transformations, and managing objects that are spawned during gameplay.

Hierarchical Scene Management

In hierarchical scene management, objects are organized into a tree structure that reflects their relationships and dependencies. For example, a character model may have a hierarchy of nodes representing its body parts, joints, and accessories. When the character moves, the entire hierarchy is transformed accordingly, maintaining the relative positions of its parts.

// Example of a simple scene graph node in C++

class SceneNode {

public:

SceneNode* parent;

std::vector<SceneNode*> children;

Transform transform;

Renderable* renderable; *// Represents the object's geometry and appearance*

};

Scene Graph Applications

Scene graphs are used in various aspects of game development:

Rendering: During rendering, the scene graph is traversed to transform objects and determine their visibility. It helps in efficient rendering of objects based on their positions and visibility.

Physics Simulation: In physics simulations, scene graphs assist in collision detection and response. Objects that are close in the hierarchy may interact physically, and their transformations need to be synchronized.

Game Logic and Interactions: Scene graphs are useful for implementing game logic and interactions. For example, a character's animations and actions can be controlled by manipulating its nodes in the hierarchy.

Level Design: Level designers often work with scene graphs to create and arrange objects in game levels. This allows them to create complex environments efficiently.

In conclusion, scene graphs and hierarchies are fundamental to managing and organizing game scenes. They provide a structured way to represent objects, their transformations, and relationships within a game world. Scene graphs play a crucial role in rendering, physics simulation, game logic, and level design, making them essential tools for game developers.

8.2 Dynamic Scene Loading and Streaming

Dynamic scene loading and streaming are essential techniques in modern game development to create vast and open game worlds while managing memory efficiently. In this section, we will explore the concepts and strategies behind dynamic scene loading and streaming.

Understanding Dynamic Scene Loading

Dynamic scene loading involves loading and unloading parts of a game world as the player navigates through it. This approach allows developers to create expansive game environments without overwhelming memory resources. There are several key components and strategies associated with dynamic scene loading:

Scene Segmentation: The game world is divided into smaller segments or chunks, each containing a portion of the environment. These chunks can be defined based on geographical features, proximity to the player, or other criteria.

Streaming Zones: Streaming zones are areas within the game world where the loading and unloading of scene chunks are triggered. Entering a new streaming zone prompts the system to load the associated chunks, and exiting unloads them.

Asynchronous Loading: Dynamic scene loading is typically asynchronous, meaning it doesn't block the game's main thread. This ensures smooth gameplay while background loading occurs.

Level of Detail (LOD): LOD techniques are often used in conjunction with dynamic scene loading. As the player moves away from a scene chunk, lower-detail versions of objects and textures can be used to save memory and processing power.

Implementation Strategies

Spatial Partitioning: Spatial partitioning techniques like octrees or grids are used to efficiently determine which scene chunks are visible and need to be loaded. This reduces unnecessary loading and unloading.

Asset Streaming: In addition to scene geometry and objects, assets like textures, audio, and scripts can also be streamed on-demand as the player explores the game world.

Memory Management: Memory is a critical resource when implementing dynamic scene loading. Efficient memory management ensures that unloaded scene chunks release memory resources appropriately.

Example in Unity (C#)

```csharp
// Example of dynamic scene loading in Unity

using UnityEngine;

using UnityEngine.SceneManagement;

public class SceneLoader : MonoBehaviour

{

public string nextSceneName;

void OnTriggerEnter(Collider other)

{

if (other.CompareTag("Player"))

{

// Load the next scene asynchronously

SceneManager.LoadSceneAsync(nextSceneName,
LoadSceneMode.Additive);

}

}

void OnTriggerExit(Collider other)

{

if (other.CompareTag("Player"))
```

```
{

// Unload the current scene asynchronously

SceneManager.UnloadSceneAsync(gameObject.scene);

}

}

}
```

In this Unity example, a script attached to a trigger volume loads the next scene when the player enters and unloads the current scene when the player exits. This dynamic loading and unloading of scenes allow for a seamless transition between areas in the game world.

Challenges and Considerations

Seamless Transitions: One of the challenges of dynamic scene loading is ensuring seamless transitions between loaded and unloaded chunks. Techniques like level streaming and preloading can help mitigate this issue.

Optimization: Efficient implementation is crucial to avoid performance hiccups during loading and unloading. Profiling and optimization are essential to achieving smooth gameplay.

Loading Screens: Depending on the complexity of scene loading, developers may need to implement loading screens or transitions to mask the process from the player.

Dynamic scene loading and streaming are powerful tools for creating expansive and immersive game worlds. When implemented effectively, they allow players to explore large and detailed environments without sacrificing performance or memory resources. However, careful planning and optimization are necessary to ensure a seamless and enjoyable gaming experience.

8.3 Level of Detail (LOD) Techniques

Level of Detail (LOD) techniques are crucial for optimizing game performance while maintaining visual quality in scenes with complex geometry. In this section, we will delve into the concept of LOD and explore various techniques used to implement it.

Understanding Level of Detail (LOD)

Level of Detail refers to the practice of using different versions or representations of an object based on its distance from the camera. Objects that are closer to the camera require high-detail models, while those farther away can use simplified or lower-detail versions. LOD is used to balance visual quality and performance.

LOD Models: LOD models are a set of progressively simplified versions of an object, each with fewer polygons and smaller textures. These models are usually pre-generated during content creation.

Transition Points: Transition points define the distances at which LOD switches occur. When an object crosses a transition point (e.g., moves closer to or farther from the camera), the appropriate LOD model is rendered.

LOD Bias: LOD bias is a factor that can be adjusted to control LOD transitions. Positive bias values make LOD transitions happen sooner, and negative values delay them. This allows fine-tuning LOD behavior.

LOD Implementation Techniques

Geometry Simplification: One of the fundamental techniques is geometry simplification. This involves reducing the number of vertices and polygons in a model. Techniques like mesh decimation and simplification algorithms can be used.

Texture Mipmapping: Mipmapping involves creating a series of progressively smaller versions of textures. When an object is rendered at a distance, a lower-resolution texture (mipmap level) is used, reducing memory and processing requirements.

Impostors: Impostors are 2D representations of 3D objects. When an object is far away, it can be replaced with a flat image that always faces the camera. Impostors are useful for distant objects like trees or billboards.

Shader Techniques: LOD can also be controlled through shaders. Shaders can adjust the level of detail in real-time based on the object's distance, screen size, or other criteria.

Example in Unity (C#)

```csharp
// Example of LOD implementation in Unity using LOD Groups

using UnityEngine;

public class LODExample : MonoBehaviour

{

public LODGroup lodGroup;

void Start()

{

// Get the LOD group component

lodGroup = GetComponent<LODGroup>();

// Create LOD levels

LOD[] lods = new LOD[3];

lods[0] = new LOD(0.2f, new Renderer[] { GetComponent<Renderer>() }); // High-detail

lods[1] = new LOD(0.5f, new Renderer[] { GetComponent<Renderer>() }); // Medium-detail

lods[2] = new LOD(1.0f, new Renderer[] { GetComponent<Renderer>() }); // Low-detail

// Assign LOD levels to the LOD group
```

```
lodGroup.SetLODs(lods);

}

}
```

In Unity, the LODGroup component allows you to define multiple LOD levels for an object. In this example, three LOD levels with varying levels of detail are defined for the object associated with the script.

Benefits and Considerations

Performance Optimization: LOD techniques significantly reduce the rendering workload, improving the game's performance, especially in scenes with many objects.

Visual Consistency: Proper LOD implementation ensures that objects transition smoothly between LOD levels, maintaining visual consistency as objects move closer or farther from the camera.

Artistic Control: LOD allows artists to balance performance and visual quality by creating LOD models and textures that match the desired aesthetic.

Complexity: Implementing LOD can be complex, particularly for objects with intricate geometry and textures. Careful planning and optimization are required.

Level of Detail is a fundamental optimization technique that helps balance visual fidelity and performance in modern games. When applied effectively, LOD techniques can result in visually stunning and highly optimized game environments, providing players with an engaging and immersive experience.

8.4 Culling Techniques

Culling techniques play a pivotal role in optimizing game rendering by determining which objects or parts of the scene should be excluded from rendering. In this section, we will explore the concept of culling and various culling techniques used in game development.

Understanding Culling

Culling is the process of eliminating objects or portions of a scene that are not visible to the camera or are outside the view frustum. The primary goal of culling is to reduce the number of objects that need to be rendered, thereby improving performance.

View Frustum: The view frustum is a geometric shape that represents the visible portion of the game world from the camera's perspective. Objects outside this shape are typically culled.

Occlusion Culling: Occlusion culling focuses on hiding objects that are completely or partially obscured by other objects. This is crucial for optimizing scenes with complex geometry.

Culling Hierarchy: Culling can be performed using spatial data structures like octrees, grids, or bounding volume hierarchies. These structures help quickly determine which objects are visible.

Culling Techniques

Frustum Culling: Frustum culling involves checking if objects are inside the view frustum. Objects entirely outside the frustum are excluded from rendering.

Backface Culling: Backface culling discards triangles that are facing away from the camera. This is effective for objects without thickness, like flat surfaces.

Occlusion Culling: Occlusion culling identifies objects that are completely hidden by other objects and skips rendering them. Techniques include portal-based culling and occlusion queries.

Distance Culling: Objects that are too far from the camera are culled based on a distance threshold. This is common for large open-world games.

LOD-Based Culling: Level of Detail (LOD) culling determines LOD levels for objects based on their distance from the camera. Distant objects use lower LODs.

Example in Unity (C#)

```csharp
// Example of frustum culling in Unity

using UnityEngine;

public class FrustumCullingExample : MonoBehaviour
{

void Update()
{

// Check if the object is within the camera's view frustum
```

```
if
(GeometryUtility.TestPlanesAABB(GeometryUtility.CalculateFrustumPlan

GetComponent<Renderer>().bounds))

{

// Object is inside the frustum, render it

GetComponent<Renderer>().enabled = true;

}

else

{

// Object is outside the frustum, disable rendering

GetComponent<Renderer>().enabled = false;

}

}

}
```

In this Unity example, the TestPlanesAABB function is used to check if the object's bounding box is within the camera's view frustum. If the object is inside the frustum, rendering is enabled; otherwise, rendering is disabled.

Benefits and Considerations

Performance Optimization: Culling reduces the number of objects that need to be rendered, resulting in improved frame rates and smoother gameplay.

Efficient Use of Resources: By excluding non-visible objects, culling techniques help conserve memory and GPU resources.

Complexity: Implementing culling can be complex, especially in scenes with dynamic objects and changing visibility conditions.

Artistic Considerations: Care must be taken to ensure that important gameplay elements are not inadvertently culled, leading to unintended consequences.

Culling techniques are fundamental for optimizing rendering in games. They are essential for achieving high performance, especially in scenes with large and complex environments. Properly implemented culling can significantly enhance the player's experience by ensuring smooth and responsive gameplay.

8.5 Spatial Partitioning and Octrees

Spatial partitioning is a vital technique in game development used to efficiently manage and query objects within a game world. In this section, we'll explore the concept of spatial partitioning, focusing on octrees as a popular spatial data structure.

Understanding Spatial Partitioning

Spatial partitioning involves dividing the game world into smaller regions or volumes, often referred to as cells or nodes. Each cell contains a subset of objects from the world. The primary purpose of spatial partitioning is to accelerate object queries, such as collision detection and visibility checks, by reducing the number of objects that need to be considered.

Benefits of Spatial Partitioning:

- **Efficient Queries**: Spatial partitioning allows for efficient queries by narrowing down the search space to only objects within the same cell or nearby cells.

- **Reduced Complexity**: Instead of comparing every object to every other object, spatial partitioning reduces the number of comparisons, improving performance.

- **Dynamic Worlds**: It accommodates dynamic worlds where objects move or change position over time.

Octrees as a Spatial Data Structure

An octree is a tree-based spatial data structure that divides 3D space into eight equal octants. Each octant can be further subdivided into eight sub-octants, creating a hierarchical structure. Octrees are commonly used in games for various purposes, including collision detection, visibility determination, and frustum culling.

Hierarchy: An octree's hierarchical structure allows for efficient traversal and subdivision of space as needed.

Objects in Nodes: Each node of the octree contains objects that are entirely contained within it. Objects near the boundary of a node may exist in multiple nodes.

Traversal: Traversing an octree involves descending the hierarchy, starting from the root node and navigating to the appropriate child nodes based on the object's position.

Example: Octree in Collision Detection

```cpp
// Example of an octree data structure for collision detection in C++

#include <vector>

struct BoundingBox {

// Represents an axis-aligned bounding box

float minX, maxX, minY, maxY, minZ, maxZ;

};

struct OctreeNode {

BoundingBox bounds;

std::vector<Object> objects;

OctreeNode* children[8];

};

class Octree {
```

public:

Octree(BoundingBox worldBounds, int maxDepth);

void Insert(Object object);

void Query(BoundingBox region, std::vector<Object>& result);

private:

OctreeNode* root;

int maxDepth;

};

In this C++ example, an octree data structure is implemented for collision detection. The octree is composed of nodes, each containing objects and subdivided into eight child nodes. Objects are inserted based on their bounding boxes, and queries can efficiently find objects within a specified region.

Benefits and Considerations

Efficient Queries: Octrees enable efficient queries for collision detection and spatial queries, making them suitable for physics engines and spatial indexing.

Dynamic Environments: Octrees can adapt to dynamic environments where objects move or change position.

Memory Overhead: Octrees consume memory to store the hierarchical structure, which can be significant for large worlds.

Complexity: Implementing and maintaining octrees can be

complex, particularly when dealing with dynamic objects and balancing tree structure.

Spatial partitioning, particularly using octrees, is a versatile technique that greatly aids in optimizing game performance and enabling efficient spatial queries. When used appropriately, it can significantly enhance collision detection, visibility determination, and other spatial operations in a game world.

Chapter 9: Advanced Animation Techniques

9.1 Skeletal Animation

Skeletal animation is a widely used technique in game development for bringing characters and creatures to life. In this section, we'll delve into the fundamentals of skeletal animation, including bones, joints, and the process of animating complex 3D models.

Understanding Skeletal Animation

Skeletal animation, also known as rigging, involves animating 3D models by defining a hierarchical structure of bones or joints that deform the model. These bones act as a skeleton for the model and are manipulated to create animations.

Bones and Joints: Bones are often used interchangeably with joints in skeletal animation. Each bone/joint has a transformation, including position, rotation, and scale.

Hierarchical Structure: Bones are organized in a hierarchy, with a root bone at the top. The hierarchy allows for complex animations by combining the transformations of parent and child bones.

Vertex Skinning: In vertex skinning, each vertex of the 3D model is associated with one or more bones, known as bone influences. The transformations of these bones affect the vertex's position.

Animation Process

The process of skeletal animation involves several key steps:

1. **Rigging**: The 3D model is prepared for animation by adding bones/joints and assigning vertices to these bones.
2. **Keyframing**: Animators define keyframes at specific times, setting bone transformations (position, rotation, scale) to create poses.
3. **Interpolation**: Between keyframes, the animation system calculates intermediate poses by interpolating between the keyframes' bone transformations.
4. **Skinning**: During rendering, the model's vertices are transformed according to the bone transformations. This is called skinning or vertex blending.

Example in Unity (C#)

```csharp
// Example of playing a skeletal animation in Unity

using UnityEngine;

public class SkeletalAnimationExample : MonoBehaviour

{

public AnimationClip animationClip;

private Animator animator;

void Start()

{

// Initialize the animator and assign the animation clip

animator = GetComponent<Animator>();

animator.Play(animationClip.name);

}
```

}

In this Unity example, an animation clip is played on a character with an Animator component. The animator handles the playback of skeletal animations defined in the animation clip.

Benefits and Considerations

Realistic Character Animation: Skeletal animation allows for realistic and expressive character animations, including walking, running, and complex facial expressions.

Efficiency: It's computationally efficient because it only requires the transformation of bones, not every vertex of the model.

Complexity: Creating a rig and animations can be complex, especially for characters with many bones and intricate movements.

Performance: Real-time playback of complex skeletal animations can be demanding on system resources.

Skeletal animation is a fundamental technique in game development that empowers developers to create lifelike character animations. Understanding the hierarchy of bones, keyframing, interpolation, and vertex skinning is essential for bringing characters and creatures to life in games.

9.2 Morph Target Animation

Morph target animation, also known as blend shape animation or vertex animation, is a technique used to animate 3D models by interpolating between different vertex positions. Unlike skeletal animation, which deforms a model using bones and joints, morph target animation directly manipulates the model's vertices to achieve animations.

Understanding Morph Target Animation

In morph target animation, a 3D model typically has a set of predefined "target" shapes or states. Each target shape represents a specific pose or deformation of the model. These targets are also known as "morph targets" or "blend shapes."

Vertex Positions: For each target shape, the positions of all vertices in the model are stored.

Interpolation: To create an animation, the system interpolates (blends) between the vertex positions of multiple targets. The interpolation is controlled by a weight or influence factor.

Linear Blend: The simplest form of interpolation is linear blending, where the vertex positions of targets are combined linearly based on the influence factor.

Animation Process

The process of morph target animation involves several steps:

1. **Creation of Targets**: The artist creates target shapes, typically representing different facial expressions, character emotions, or deformations.
2. **Keyframing**: Animators define keyframes by specifying the weights or influences of each target shape at specific times in the animation.
3. **Interpolation**: Between keyframes, the system smoothly

interpolates the weights of the target shapes. This interpolation creates the illusion of continuous deformation.

4. **Vertex Deformation**: During rendering, the model's vertices are deformed based on the interpolated weights of the target shapes.

Example in Unity (C#)

```csharp
// Example of morph target animation in Unity

using UnityEngine;

public class MorphTargetAnimation : MonoBehaviour
{

public SkinnedMeshRenderer meshRenderer;

public Mesh[] morphTargets;

private int currentMorphTargetIndex = 0;

void Update()
{

// Switch between morph targets over time

if (Input.GetKeyDown(KeyCode.Space))
{

currentMorphTargetIndex = (currentMorphTargetIndex + 1) % morphTargets.Length;

meshRenderer.sharedMesh = morphTargets[currentMorphTargetIndex];
```

```
}

}

}
```

In this Unity example, morph target animation is achieved by switching between different meshes (morph targets) at runtime. This creates the appearance of animated deformation or facial expressions.

Benefits and Considerations

Artistic Control: Morph target animation offers precise control over specific deformations, making it suitable for facial expressions and shape-based animations.

Performance: It can be computationally efficient, as it doesn't require complex bone hierarchies and transformations.

Limitations: Morph target animation is best suited for specific animations like facial expressions and shape changes. It may not be ideal for complex character movements.

Memory Usage: Storing multiple morph targets can consume memory, especially for high-resolution models.

Morph target animation is a valuable technique for achieving specific character animations, especially for facial expressions and shape-based deformations. It provides artists and animators with granular control over the appearance of a 3D model during animations, allowing for highly detailed and expressive character performances.

9.3 Dynamic and Destructible Environments

Dynamic and destructible environments are exciting features in modern game development. They allow players to interact with and impact the game world, creating a more immersive and engaging experience. In this section, we'll explore the concepts and techniques behind dynamic and destructible environments.

Dynamic Environments

Dynamic environments refer to game worlds that change or react in response to various factors, including player actions, in-game events, or even external influences like weather and time of day. These environments enhance gameplay by creating a sense of realism and unpredictability.

Physics Simulation: Dynamic environments often rely on physics simulation to determine how objects, characters, and elements interact with each other and the world. Physics engines like NVIDIA PhysX and Havok are commonly used for this purpose.

Examples: Dynamic environments can include things like destructible objects (e.g., buildings that can be destroyed), dynamic weather systems, day-night cycles, and changing terrain (e.g., erosion and terrain deformation).

Gameplay Impact: Dynamic environments can significantly impact gameplay by offering new challenges, opportunities, and emergent gameplay experiences. For example, changing weather conditions may affect visibility and mobility.

Destructible Environments

Destructible environments take dynamic environments a step further by allowing players to damage or destroy objects and structures within the game world. This feature is often used in action-packed games to create intense and immersive combat scenarios.

Physics-Based Destruction: Destructible environments typically use physics-based algorithms to simulate how objects break apart and react to forces. This involves calculating fractures, debris, and the effects of explosions.

Gameplay Variety: Destructible environments add variety to gameplay by enabling players to use the environment as a weapon or as cover. For example, players might strategically destroy a bridge to impede enemy progress.

Challenges: Implementing destructible environments can be technically challenging due to the complexity of physics simulations and the need to balance realism with gameplay.

Techniques and Tools

Developers use various techniques and tools to implement dynamic and destructible environments:

- **Physics Engines**: Utilizing third-party physics engines or in-house solutions to handle realistic object interactions.

- **Mesh Deformation**: Modifying 3D models in real-time to simulate damage and deformation.

- **Particle Systems**: Creating particle effects for explosions, dust, and debris when objects break apart.

- **Scripting**: Writing scripts to control the behavior of destructible objects and environmental changes.

- **Level Design**: Careful level design to ensure that destructible elements are strategically placed to enhance gameplay.

- **Sound Effects**: Adding audio cues to enhance the immersive experience, such as the sound of crumbling buildings.

Example in Unreal Engine (Blueprints)

```
// Example of destructible environment in Unreal Engine using Blueprints

OnCollisionEnter(Event)

{

if (Event.impactForce > 1000)

{

DestroyMesh(); // Destroy the mesh when impacted with sufficient force

}

}
```

In this Unreal Engine example, a destructible environment is created using Blueprints. When an object collides with sufficient force, the mesh is destroyed, providing a dynamic and interactive environment.

Dynamic and destructible environments can significantly enhance the player's experience by allowing them to impact and interact with the game world. These features require careful design, physics simulation, and scripting to create immersive and engaging gameplay scenarios.

9.4 Real-time IK (Inverse Kinematics)

Real-time Inverse Kinematics (IK) is a powerful technique used in game development to animate characters and objects realistically by solving the problem of determining joint positions to reach a desired end-effector position. In this section, we will delve into the concept of real-time IK and its applications in game development.

Understanding Inverse Kinematics

Inverse Kinematics is the opposite of Forward Kinematics, which is often used to calculate the final position of an end-effector (e.g., a character's hand) given joint angles. Inverse Kinematics, on the other hand, calculates joint angles to position the end-effector where you want it to be.

Example: Think of a character's arm. Forward Kinematics would help you find the hand's position based on the shoulder, elbow, and wrist joint angles. Inverse Kinematics, on the contrary, would determine the joint angles required to place the hand at a specific location in 3D space.

Applications in Game Development

Inverse Kinematics finds a wide range of applications in game development:

Character Animation: Realistic character animations, such as walking, running, and climbing, can be achieved by using IK to control the character's limbs and body movements.

Environmental Interaction: IK allows characters to interact with the environment dynamically, like picking up objects, grabbing ledges, or climbing stairs smoothly.

Procedural Animation: In procedural animation systems, IK can create lifelike animations that respond to the game's dynamic conditions, such as a character adjusting their balance on uneven terrain.

Solving IK Problems

Solving IK problems typically involves numerical methods like the Jacobian Transpose method or the Cyclic Coordinate Descent (CCD) algorithm. These methods iteratively adjust joint angles until the end-effector reaches the desired position.

Unity Example (C#)

```csharp
// Example of using Unity's IK system (AimIK) to make a character aim at a target.

using UnityEngine;

using RootMotion.FinalIK; // Import the IK library

public class AimAtTarget : MonoBehaviour
{

public AimIK aimIK; // Reference to the AimIK component
```

```
public Transform target; // The target to aim at

void Update()

{

// Set the target position for the IK solver

aimIK.solver.IKPosition = target.position;

}

}
```

In this Unity example, the AimIK component is used to make a character aim at a target in real-time. The IK solver adjusts the character's arm joints to aim at the specified target position.

Challenges and Considerations

Implementing real-time IK in games can be challenging due to its computational cost and the need for careful tuning. Here are some considerations:

- **Performance**: Real-time IK calculations can be resource-intensive, so optimization is crucial for maintaining a smooth frame rate.

- **Joint Limits**: Ensuring that joint limits are respected to prevent unnatural contortions.

- **Blending**: Integrating IK seamlessly with other animation systems and blending between IK and traditional animations.

Real-time IK is a powerful tool for achieving lifelike character animations and interactions in games. While it comes with challenges, it opens up possibilities for creating more dynamic and immersive gameplay experiences.

9.5 Facial Animation and Lip Sync

Facial animation and lip sync are essential aspects of character animation in games, contributing to a character's expressiveness and realism. In this section, we will explore the techniques and tools used to bring characters' faces to life in games.

Facial Animation Techniques

Blend Shapes (Morph Targets): Blend shapes involve creating a set of predefined facial expressions and interpolating between them to create a wide range of facial animations. Each shape represents a specific facial feature like a smile, frown, or raised eyebrow.

Bone-Based Rigging: Bone-based facial rigs use a system of bones and joints to control facial expressions. This approach allows for more complex and dynamic facial animations, including realistic eye and mouth movement.

Facial Capture: Facial capture involves recording an actor's facial expressions and mapping them onto a 3D character model. This technique results in highly realistic facial animations but can be computationally expensive.

Lip Sync

Lip sync is the synchronization of a character's lip movements with the spoken dialogue or audio. Achieving convincing lip sync is crucial for making in-game characters appear realistic when they speak. Here are common approaches to lip sync:

Phoneme-Based Animation: This method involves creating a set of phonemes (distinct mouth shapes for different sounds) and transitioning between them based on the phonetics of the spoken words.

Audio Analysis: Lip sync can be automated by analyzing the audio waveform and matching it with predefined lip movement animations. This approach is less time-consuming but may require manual adjustments for accuracy.

Performance Capture: Similar to facial capture, performance capture involves recording an actor's facial movements and speech simultaneously. This results in highly realistic lip sync but requires specialized equipment.

Tools for Facial Animation

Game developers use various tools and software for facial animation and lip sync:

- **3D Animation Software**: Tools like Autodesk Maya, Blender, and 3ds Max are commonly used for creating facial animations and rigs.

- **Facial Animation Software**: Specific software like Faceware and FaceFX provides tools for facial capture and lip sync.

- **Game Engines**: Game engines like Unity and Unreal Engine have built-in features and plugins for facial animation and lip sync.

Unity Example (C#)

```csharp
// Example of setting up lip sync in Unity using the LipSync Pro plugin.

using UnityEngine;

using RogoDigital.Lipsync; // Import the LipSync Pro library

public class LipSyncController : MonoBehaviour

{

public LipSyncData lipsyncData; // Reference to the lip sync data asset

public LipSync lipsync; // Reference to the LipSync component

void Start()

{

// Load the lip sync data

lipsync.Load(lipsyncData);

}

void Update()

{

// Play lip sync based on audio input or dialog

if (Input.GetKeyDown(KeyCode.Space))
```

```
{

lipsync.Play(lipsyncData);

}

}

}
```

In this Unity example, the LipSync Pro plugin is used to set up lip sync for a character. The script loads lip sync data and plays it when triggered, synchronizing the character's lip movements with the provided audio data.

Facial animation and lip sync are essential for bringing characters to life in games. These techniques, combined with advanced animation tools and software, allow game developers to create emotionally expressive and realistic characters that enhance the overall gaming experience.

Chapter 10: Real-time Ray Tracing

Section 10.1: Basics of Ray Tracing

Ray tracing is a rendering technique that simulates the way rays of light interact with objects in a scene to generate highly realistic images. Unlike rasterization, which is the traditional rendering method used in real-time graphics, ray tracing can produce more accurate and visually stunning results. In this section, we will delve into the fundamentals of ray tracing and how it is implemented in real-time graphics.

Ray Tracing Concepts

1. **Ray Generation**: Ray tracing begins with the generation of primary rays. These rays are cast from the camera's viewpoint into the scene. Each primary ray represents a pixel on the screen.
2. **Intersection Testing**: For each primary ray, ray tracing checks for intersections with objects in the scene. This involves determining if and where the ray hits an object's surface.
3. **Shading and Lighting**: Once an intersection is found, ray tracing calculates the lighting and shading at that point on the object's surface. This includes handling reflections, refractions, and global illumination.
4. **Secondary Rays**: Ray tracing often involves casting secondary rays, such as reflection rays and shadow rays, to simulate complex lighting interactions.
5. **Recursive Ray Tracing**: When a ray encounters a reflective or refractive surface, it can spawn new rays, resulting in recursive ray tracing. This is essential for handling reflections and transparency.

Real-time Ray Tracing Challenges

Real-time ray tracing presents several challenges due to its computational intensity. Achieving high frame rates while performing complex ray tracing calculations requires specialized hardware and optimization techniques.

1. **Hardware Acceleration**: Modern GPUs and specialized hardware like NVIDIA's RTX series include dedicated ray tracing cores to accelerate ray tracing operations.

2. **Bounding Volume Hierarchy (BVH)**: BVH is a data structure used to optimize ray-object intersection tests by reducing the number of checks.

3. **Parallelism**: Ray tracing benefits from parallel processing, and GPUs are well-suited for this task. Implementing parallel algorithms is crucial for real-time ray tracing performance.

4. **Dynamic Scenes**: Handling dynamic scenes with moving objects or changing lighting conditions requires efficient updates to the ray tracing data structures.

5. **Level of Detail (LOD)**: LOD techniques are used to simplify ray tracing calculations for distant objects or areas of the scene that are less visible.

Ray Tracing in Game Engines

Game engines like Unreal Engine and Unity have integrated support for real-time ray tracing. They provide tools and APIs that allow developers to utilize ray tracing features in their games, including ray-traced reflections, shadows, and ambient occlusion.

```
// Pseudo code for ray tracing pseudorandom ray generation

for (pixel in screen) {

// Generate a primary ray from the camera

Ray primaryRay = GeneratePrimaryRay(pixel);

// Check for intersections with objects in the scene

Intersection intersection = Trace(primaryRay, scene);

if (intersection.hit) {
```

```
// Calculate shading and lighting at the intersection point
Color pixelColor = Shade(intersection, scene);
// Set the pixel color in the frame buffer
frameBuffer[pixel] = pixelColor;
} else {
// Set a background color if no intersection is found
frameBuffer[pixel] = backgroundColor;
}
}
```

This pseudocode demonstrates the basic ray tracing process, where primary rays are generated for each pixel, intersections are tested, and shading is applied to determine the final pixel color. Real-time ray tracing builds upon this foundation to create visually stunning game graphics with realistic lighting and reflections.

Section 10.2: Ray Tracing in OpenGL

Ray tracing is a powerful rendering technique, but traditionally, it has been computationally expensive and not suitable for real-time applications. However, with recent advancements in hardware and the development of ray tracing APIs like NVIDIA's RTX and Microsoft's DirectX Raytracing (DXR), it has become feasible to implement real-time ray tracing in game engines using OpenGL.

OpenGL and Ray Tracing

OpenGL is a widely used graphics API known for its versatility and cross-platform support. While it has primarily been associated with rasterization-based rendering, recent extensions and libraries have allowed developers to integrate ray tracing into OpenGL applications.

Extensions and Libraries

1. **NVIDIA RTX**: NVIDIA's RTX series GPUs introduce hardware support for ray tracing, making it possible to offload ray tracing calculations from the CPU to the GPU.
2. **Vulkan**: Vulkan is another graphics API that supports ray tracing through extensions like VK_KHR_ray_tracing.
3. **OptiX**: NVIDIA's OptiX is a ray tracing framework that provides a high-level API for ray tracing applications. It can be integrated with OpenGL for real-time ray tracing.

Ray Tracing Shaders

In OpenGL, ray tracing is implemented using specialized shaders known as ray tracing shaders. These shaders allow developers to define how rays are generated, traced, and interact with the scene.

Ray Generation Shader

The ray generation shader is the entry point for ray tracing. It defines how primary rays are generated, typically from the camera's viewpoint, and how they traverse the scene. Here's an example of a simple ray generation shader in GLSL:

```
#version 460 core
```

```
layout(location = 0) buffer image2D outputBuffer;

void main() {

ivec2 pixelCoords = ivec2(gl_GlobalInvocationID.xy);

vec2 normalizedCoords = (vec2(pixelCoords) + vec2(0.5)) / imageSize(outputBuffer);

// Calculate the ray direction based on the pixel coordinates

// Ray tracing logic goes here

// Trace the ray and calculate the pixel color

vec3 pixelColor = TraceRay(ray);

// Store the pixel color in the output buffer

imageStore(outputBuffer, pixelCoords, vec4(pixelColor, 1.0));

}
```

Ray Intersection Shader

Ray intersection shaders are used to test whether a ray intersects with objects in the scene. These shaders are responsible for calculating intersection points and material properties. Here's a simplified example:

```
hitAttributeEXT vec3 hitColor;

void main() {

// Calculate intersection logic

// Compute the intersection point, normal, and material properties
```

```
// Set the hit attributes

hitColor = intersectedColor;

gl_HitEXT = true;

}
```

Ray Miss Shader

The ray miss shader defines what happens when a ray doesn't hit any objects in the scene. It's often used to set background colors or handle skyboxes.

```
void main() {

// Set the background color or skybox texture

// based on the ray direction

// ...

}
```

Ray Tracing Pipeline

In OpenGL, ray tracing shaders are organized into a pipeline, similar to how vertex and fragment shaders are organized in a rasterization pipeline. The pipeline includes the ray generation shader, intersection shaders, and miss shaders. It's configured using OpenGL API calls and used to trace rays and generate the final image.

Performance Considerations

Real-time ray tracing in OpenGL can be demanding on hardware. To achieve good performance, developers should consider techniques like acceleration structures (e.g., BVH), shader optimizations, and using hardware ray tracing support when available.

```
// Pseudo code for setting up a ray tracing pipeline in OpenGL

// (using the NVIDIA RTX extension for simplicity)

// Create ray tracing shader modules

GLuint rayGenShader = CreateShaderModule(rayGenGLSL);

GLuint missShader = CreateShaderModule(missGLSL);

GLuint hitShader = CreateShaderModule(hitGLSL);

// Create a ray tracing pipeline

GLuint rayTracingPipeline;

glCreateRayTracingPipelinesNV(1, &rayTracingPipeline, ...);

glRayTracingPipelineShaderGroupNV(rayTracingPipeline,        0,
rayGenShader);

glRayTracingPipelineShaderGroupNV(rayTracingPipeline,        1,
missShader);

glRayTracingPipelineShaderGroupNV(rayTracingPipeline,        2,
hitShader);

// Trace rays and generate the final image

glBindRayTracingPipelineNV(GL_RAY_TRACING_SHADER_GROU
rayTracingPipeline);

glDispatchRaysNV(...);
```

This pseudocode illustrates the setup of a ray tracing pipeline in OpenGL using the NVIDIA RTX extension. It highlights the key components and stages involved in real-time ray tracing integration with OpenGL. Developers can fine-tune and optimize their ray tracing pipelines based on their specific requirements and hardware capabilities.

Section 10.3: Reflections, Refractions, and Caustics

Ray tracing in OpenGL opens up possibilities for rendering advanced optical effects like reflections, refractions, and caustics. These effects simulate the behavior of light as it interacts with surfaces and materials in the virtual environment, creating realistic and visually appealing scenes.

Reflections

Reflections occur when light bounces off surfaces and into the virtual camera. Implementing reflections in ray tracing involves casting secondary rays (reflection rays) from the hit point on a surface. These rays follow the law of reflection and determine what is visible in reflective surfaces.

Here's a simplified GLSL example for handling reflections:

```glsl
vec3 Reflect(vec3 incidentDir, vec3 normal) {

return incidentDir - 2.0 * dot(incidentDir, normal) * normal;

}

// Inside the main ray tracing loop

vec3 ReflectiveSurface(ray) {
```

```glsl
// Calculate the intersection point and normal
// ...
vec3 reflectionRayDir = Reflect(ray.direction, normal);
vec3 reflectionColor = TraceRay(reflectionRay);
// Combine reflectionColor with the surface's material properties
vec3 finalColor = reflectionColor * surfaceColor;
return finalColor;
}
```

Refractions

Refractions occur when light passes from one material into another with a different refractive index, causing the light to change direction. Implementing refractions in ray tracing involves casting refraction rays and calculating their intersections with transparent materials.

Here's a simplified GLSL example for handling refractions:

```glsl
vec3 Refract(vec3 incidentDir, vec3 normal, float eta) {
float cosThetaI = dot(incidentDir, normal);
float sinThetaI = sqrt(max(0.0, 1.0 - cosThetaI * cosThetaI));
float sinThetaT = eta * sinThetaI;
float cosThetaT = sqrt(max(0.0, 1.0 - sinThetaT * sinThetaT));
return eta * incidentDir + (eta * cosThetaI - cosThetaT) * normal;
}
```

```
// Inside the main ray tracing loop

vec3 TransparentMaterial(ray) {

// Calculate the intersection point and normal

// ...

float eta = 1.5; // Refractive index of the material

vec3 refractionRayDir = Refract(ray.direction, normal, eta);

vec3 refractionColor = TraceRay(refractionRay);

// Combine refractionColor with the surface's material properties

vec3 finalColor = refractionColor * surfaceColor;

return finalColor;

}
```

Caustics

Caustics are intricate light patterns formed when light is concentrated or focused by reflective or refractive surfaces. They are common in scenes with water, glass, or other transparent materials. Achieving realistic caustics in ray tracing involves complex calculations and photon mapping techniques.

While implementing caustics is beyond the scope of a simple example, it typically involves:

1. **Photon Mapping**: Simulating the paths of photons as they interact with surfaces, get refracted, and contribute to caustic patterns.
2. **Photon Tracing**: Tracing photons from light sources and

storing their interactions with surfaces in a photon map.

3. **Gathering Photons**: When rendering a scene, gather photons from the photon map to calculate caustic effects on surfaces.

Advanced ray tracing frameworks and libraries often provide tools and algorithms for handling caustics, as it requires substantial computational resources and optimization.

In summary, ray tracing in OpenGL allows for the implementation of advanced optical effects like reflections, refractions, and caustics. These effects enhance the realism and visual quality of rendered scenes, making ray tracing a valuable technique for computer graphics and game development. Developers can adapt and extend these concepts to create stunning visual experiences in their applications.

Section 10.4: Ray Traced Shadows

Ray-traced shadows are an essential component of realistic rendering in ray tracing. Shadows add depth, dimension, and believability to scenes by accurately simulating how objects block light sources. In this section, we will explore the implementation of ray-traced shadows in OpenGL.

Basic Shadow Ray Casting

The fundamental idea behind ray-traced shadows is to cast shadow rays from a point of interest (typically a camera or a reflection/ refraction point) toward each light source in the scene. If a shadow ray hits any object before reaching the light source, the point is in shadow; otherwise, it is illuminated.

Here's a simplified GLSL example for implementing shadow ray casting:

```
bool IsInShadow(vec3 point, vec3 lightDir) {

// Cast a ray from 'point' towards the light source

Ray shadowRay;

shadowRay.origin = point + 0.001 * normal; // Slightly offset to avoid self-intersection

shadowRay.direction = lightDir;

// Check for intersections with scene geometry

float t;

if (IntersectScene(shadowRay, t)) {

// An intersection occurred; the point is in shadow

return true;

}

// No intersections; the point is illuminated

return false;

}

// Inside the main ray tracing loop

vec3 CalculateLightContribution(vec3 point, vec3 normal, vec3 lightDir) {

// Check if the point is in shadow
```

```
bool inShadow = IsInShadow(point, lightDir);

if (inShadow) {

// The point is in shadow; no direct light contribution

return vec3(0.0);

} else {

// The point is illuminated; calculate lighting

// ...

}

}
```

Soft Shadows

To create more realistic and soft shadows, you can introduce randomness into the shadow ray directions when casting rays to light sources. This randomization is achieved using techniques like jittered sampling or area light source sampling. By sampling multiple shadow rays within the area of the light source, you can simulate the softening effect of light.

Ray Traced Hard Shadows

In the case of hard shadows, you can use a single shadow ray to determine if a point is in shadow or not. Hard shadows are characterized by well-defined, sharp shadow boundaries and are commonly used in scenes with strong direct lighting.

Performance Considerations

Implementing ray-traced shadows in OpenGL can be computationally expensive, especially in scenes with many light sources and complex geometry. To improve performance, developers often use acceleration structures like BVH (Bounding Volume Hierarchy) or spatial data structures to efficiently find potential intersections during shadow ray casting.

In conclusion, ray-traced shadows are a crucial element in achieving realism in ray tracing. By casting shadow rays from points of interest towards light sources, developers can simulate the blocking of light and create visually appealing shadows in their scenes. Techniques like soft shadows and performance optimizations further enhance the quality and efficiency of ray-traced shadow rendering.

Section 10.5: Performance Considerations and Optimization

Ray tracing is a computationally intensive rendering technique, and achieving real-time performance can be a significant challenge. In this section, we'll explore various performance considerations and optimization techniques for real-time ray tracing in OpenGL.

1. GPU Acceleration

One of the key optimizations for ray tracing is leveraging the power of modern GPUs. Graphics cards are highly parallel processors and can perform ray intersection tests much faster than CPUs. To utilize GPU acceleration, developers often use compute shaders or dedicated ray tracing hardware available in modern GPUs.

2. BVH (Bounding Volume Hierarchy)

Bounding Volume Hierarchies are spatial data structures that help optimize ray-object intersection tests. BVHs partition the scene into hierarchical bounding volumes, reducing the number of objects that need to be tested for intersection. BVH construction and traversal can be efficiently parallelized on the GPU, making it a popular choice for ray tracing acceleration.

3. Ray Coherence and Caching

In real-time ray tracing, rays are often coherent, meaning neighboring pixels or rays from the same source tend to follow similar paths through the scene. Exploiting this coherence can improve performance by caching intersection results and reusing them for neighboring rays.

4. Denoising Techniques

Ray tracing can produce noisy images, especially in complex scenes with limited samples per pixel. Denoising algorithms, such as temporal reprojection and machine learning-based methods, can be applied to reduce noise while maintaining image quality. Denoising is crucial for achieving smooth and visually pleasing results in real-time ray tracing.

5. Screen Space Techniques

Screen space techniques can help reduce the computational load in ray tracing. For example, screen space reflections (SSR) limit ray tracing to pixels visible on the screen, skipping objects that are not visible in the current view. Similarly, screen space ambient occlusion (SSAO) can be used to approximate global illumination effects more efficiently.

6. Level of Detail (LOD)

In scenes with complex geometry, it's essential to manage the level of detail based on the distance from the camera. LOD techniques reduce the number of rays cast and intersection tests performed for distant objects, improving overall performance.

7. Ray Reordering

Reordering rays can improve cache efficiency during ray tracing. Techniques like Morton ordering or Hilbert ordering reorganize rays to minimize memory access latency, leading to faster traversal of acceleration structures and improved ray-object intersection performance.

8. Asynchronous Ray Tracing

Asynchronous ray tracing allows ray tracing workloads to run in parallel with other rendering tasks. By interleaving ray tracing with traditional rasterization or shading operations, you can achieve better overall frame rates and responsiveness.

9. Profiling and Optimization Tools

Profiling tools and performance analysis are invaluable for identifying bottlenecks in ray tracing applications. Tools like NVIDIA Nsight, AMD Radeon GPU Profiler, and Intel VTune Profiler can help pinpoint performance issues and guide optimization efforts.

10. Render Resolution and Ray Depth

Reducing the render resolution and limiting ray recursion depth can significantly improve performance. This approach sacrifices some image quality for better frame rates and is often used in real-time applications.

In conclusion, real-time ray tracing in OpenGL is a challenging but rewarding endeavor. By employing GPU acceleration, spatial data structures like BVHs, and various optimization techniques, developers can achieve impressive visual quality while maintaining acceptable frame rates. Profiling and profiling tools are essential for identifying performance bottlenecks and guiding optimization efforts in real-time ray tracing projects.

Chapter 11: Physically-Based Rendering (PBR)

Section 11.1: Introduction to PBR

Physically-Based Rendering (PBR) is a rendering technique that aims to simulate real-world materials and lighting in computer graphics. It has gained significant popularity in the game development and computer graphics communities for its ability to create highly realistic and visually appealing scenes.

PBR is based on the principles of physics, particularly the behavior of light interacting with different materials. It provides a more accurate and intuitive way to model materials, making it easier for artists and developers to create lifelike virtual worlds. In traditional rendering models, materials were often represented using ad-hoc parameters that did not necessarily correlate with real-world properties. PBR, on the other hand, strives to use physically accurate parameters.

Key Concepts in PBR

1. Microsurface Theory

PBR begins with the concept of microsurfaces. It models the surface of materials as being composed of countless microfacets, each of which can reflect and refract light independently. The distribution of these microfacets affects how light interacts with the material.

- **Roughness**: This parameter defines how rough or smooth the microsurface is. Rough surfaces scatter light in many directions, creating diffuse reflections, while smooth surfaces produce sharper specular highlights.

- **Fresnel-Schlick Approximation**: The Fresnel-Schlick approximation is used to describe how materials become more reflective at glancing angles. This simulates phenomena like reflection and refraction.

2. Metallic and Specular Workflow

In PBR, materials are classified as either metals or dielectrics (non-metals). Metals exhibit conductive behavior, and their appearance is determined by their reflection color. Dielectrics, on the other hand, have a specular reflection color and an underlying diffuse color.

- **Metallic**: This parameter controls whether a material is a metal (1.0) or dielectric (0.0). Values in between represent semi-metals or materials with varying degrees of metallicity.

- **Specular**: For dielectrics, this parameter defines the color of the specular reflection. For metals, it represents the reflection color.

3. Image-Based Lighting with PBR

PBR relies heavily on image-based lighting (IBL) techniques to capture real-world lighting conditions. This involves using high-dynamic-range environment maps (HDRIs) to provide accurate lighting information.

- **Irradiance Maps**: These precomputed maps capture the ambient lighting information for various directions on a surface. They are used to simulate global illumination effects.

- **Radiance Environment Maps**: These HDRIs contain information about the intensity and directionality of incoming light. They are used for specular reflections and refractions.

Advantages of PBR

- Realism: PBR produces highly realistic materials and lighting, making virtual scenes look more like their real-world counterparts.

- Artistic Control: PBR provides artists with intuitive parameters to control material properties.

- Consistency: PBR helps maintain visual consistency across different lighting conditions and environments.

- Compatibility: PBR is widely supported in modern game engines and rendering frameworks.

In the following sections, we will explore PBR in greater detail, including its implementation in OpenGL and how to integrate it into a game engine.

Section 11.2: Microsurface Theory

Microsurface theory is a fundamental concept in Physically-Based Rendering (PBR) that plays a crucial role in modeling how light interacts with materials. It forms the basis for understanding and simulating the behavior of materials in a physically accurate way.

In microsurface theory, the surface of a material is considered to be composed of countless microfacets or microsurfaces. These microfacets are tiny geometric elements that make up the visible surface. Each microfacet can reflect and refract light independently, contributing to the overall appearance of the material.

The key parameters associated with microsurface theory in PBR are:

Roughness

Roughness is a fundamental parameter that characterizes the microsurface of a material. It determines how smooth or rough the surface appears. In PBR, roughness is typically represented as a value between 0 and 1, where 0 represents a perfectly smooth surface, and 1 represents a completely rough or matte surface.

- **Smooth Surfaces (Low Roughness)**: Materials with low roughness values have microfacets that are relatively aligned and produce sharp specular reflections. These surfaces exhibit mirror-like behavior, where light is reflected at predictable angles, similar to a polished metal surface.

- **Rough Surfaces (High Roughness)**: Materials with high roughness values have microfacets that are oriented in various directions. This leads to diffuse scattering of light, resulting in a more diffuse and blurry appearance. Rough surfaces scatter incoming light in many directions, creating soft specular highlights.

Fresnel-Schlick Approximation

The Fresnel-Schlick approximation is an essential component of microsurface theory in PBR. It simulates the phenomenon where materials become more reflective at glancing angles (i.e., when viewed at shallow angles). This behavior is observed in many real-world materials, such as glass, water, and metals.

The Fresnel-Schlick approximation is used to calculate the amount of reflected light based on the viewing angle. It produces a smooth transition between the material's reflectance at normal incidence (directly facing the viewer) and its reflectance at glancing angles.

The Fresnel-Schlick approximation is defined by the following equation:

$$[F() = F\_0 + (1 - F\_0)(1 -)^\wedge 5]$$

- $(F())$ represents the reflectance at a given viewing angle ().

- (F_0) is the reflectance at normal incidence (i.e., when $(= 0)$).

- $()$ is the cosine of the viewing angle.

By using this approximation, PBR shaders can accurately model how materials' reflectance changes with viewing angles, leading to more realistic rendering of materials like glass and metals.

In practice, microsurface theory and the associated roughness and Fresnel-Schlick approximation are essential components of PBR shaders. They allow developers and artists to create materials that exhibit a wide range of surface appearances, from perfectly smooth and reflective to rough and diffuse, leading to more visually compelling and physically accurate graphics in real-time rendering applications.

Section 11.3: Metallic and Specular Workflow

In Physically-Based Rendering (PBR), the choice of workflow for modeling materials is a critical consideration. Two common workflows used in PBR are the Metallic and Specular workflows, each with its own advantages and use cases.

Metallic Workflow

The Metallic workflow is designed for materials that are primarily metals or conductive materials. In this workflow, the key parameter that defines the material's appearance is the **metallic** value. This value is typically represented as a grayscale map or a scalar value, where 0 indicates a dielectric or non-metallic material (e.g., plastic, wood), and 1 represents a fully metallic material (e.g., gold, copper).

Advantages of Metallic Workflow:

1. **Simplicity**: The Metallic workflow is straightforward to understand and implement. It requires only one key parameter, making it user-friendly for artists and developers.
2. **Energy Conservation**: It inherently conserves energy in the rendering process, ensuring that the material's reflectance properties are physically plausible.
3. **Artistic Control**: Artists have control over the balance between diffuse and specular reflections by adjusting the metallic value.

Specular Workflow

The Specular workflow, also known as the Specular-Glossiness workflow, is suitable for a wide range of materials, including both dielectrics and metals. Instead of using a metallic value, this workflow relies on two parameters: **specular color** and **glossiness**.

- **Specular Color**: Specular color defines the color of the material's specular reflection. Unlike the metallic workflow, it can represent a wide variety of materials, from non-metals to metals.

- **Glossiness**: Glossiness, often represented as a grayscale map or scalar value, determines how sharp or blurred the specular reflections are. A low glossiness value creates broad and blurry reflections, while a high glossiness value produces sharp and focused specular highlights.

Advantages of Specular Workflow:

1. **Versatility**: The Specular workflow is versatile and can handle a broad range of materials, making it suitable for a variety of scenes and objects.
2. **Artistic Control**: Artists have fine-grained control over the appearance of specular reflections by adjusting both the specular color and glossiness.
3. **Flexibility**: It allows for more complex material variations by independently controlling the color and sharpness of specular highlights.

Choosing the Right Workflow

The choice between the Metallic and Specular workflows depends on the specific requirements of a project and the materials being represented. When dealing with predominantly metallic materials, the Metallic workflow is often a more intuitive choice. However, for a diverse range of materials or artistic flexibility, the Specular workflow provides greater control.

Implementing these workflows in shaders involves considering the physics of light interaction with materials and creating shaders that accurately simulate the desired material appearance. By choosing the appropriate workflow and setting the associated parameters, developers and artists can achieve realistic and visually appealing materials in their real-time rendering applications.

Section 11.4: Image-Based Lighting with PBR

Image-Based Lighting (IBL) is a technique widely used in Physically-Based Rendering (PBR) to enhance the realism of 3D scenes by capturing and utilizing real-world lighting information. It plays a crucial role in achieving accurate and visually appealing lighting effects in computer graphics.

Capturing Environment Maps

The foundation of IBL is the use of environment maps, which are high-dynamic-range (HDR) images or cube maps representing the surrounding environment's lighting. These maps can be captured through various methods:

1. **HDR Photography**: Photographers capture multiple exposures of a scene to cover a wide range of lighting conditions. These images are then merged into an HDR panorama.
2. **3D Scanning**: Specialized 3D scanners and cameras can capture environment maps by recording light information from the physical environment.
3. **Synthetic Generation**: Environment maps can also be created synthetically using 3D modeling software or dedicated software tools. This is often done for virtual

environments.

Using Environment Maps

Once environment maps are acquired, they can be utilized in the rendering pipeline for PBR rendering:

1. **Image-Based Lighting**: Environment maps provide accurate ambient lighting information for a scene. This lighting can be used to illuminate objects indirectly, simulating the way light bounces off surfaces in the real world.

2. **Reflections**: Environment maps are used for generating reflections on surfaces. This is essential for achieving realistic and dynamic reflections in PBR materials.

3. **Refractions**: In transparent materials, such as glass, environment maps are used to simulate the bending of light as it passes through the material. This creates convincing refraction effects.

4. **Background**: Environment maps are often used as the background skybox in a 3D scene. This creates a seamless transition between 3D objects and the environment.

Importance of HDR

High-dynamic-range (HDR) environment maps are crucial for IBL because they can represent a wide range of lighting conditions, from extremely bright to very dim. This is essential for accurately simulating real-world lighting scenarios where light intensities vary greatly.

Pre-filtering and Mipmap Generation

To efficiently use environment maps in real-time rendering, pre-filtering and mipmap generation techniques are applied. These techniques create a series of pre-convolved maps at different levels of detail (mipmaps), making the sampling process more efficient and reducing aliasing artifacts.

Dynamic IBL

In modern game engines, dynamic IBL is achieved by updating environment maps in real-time based on changes in the scene or lighting conditions. This allows for interactive and dynamic lighting effects, enhancing the realism of the rendered scene.

Conclusion

Image-Based Lighting is a fundamental component of PBR rendering, providing accurate and realistic lighting effects in computer graphics. Capturing, processing, and utilizing environment maps allow for the creation of visually stunning 3D scenes that closely mimic the behavior of light in the real world. Whether for games, simulations, or architectural visualization, IBL significantly contributes to the quality and immersion of rendered environments.

Section 11.5: Integrating PBR into a Game Engine

Integrating Physically-Based Rendering (PBR) into a game engine is a complex but rewarding task. PBR enhances the realism of rendered scenes by simulating the physical behavior of light, materials, and surfaces. Here, we'll discuss the key steps and considerations when integrating PBR into a game engine.

1. Shader Development

PBR relies on complex shaders that accurately model the interaction between light and materials. You'll need to develop shaders that support various PBR workflows, such as the metallic-roughness and specular-glossiness models. These shaders should handle lighting equations, reflections, refractions, and more.

```
// Example PBR shader pseudocode

void main() {

// Lighting calculations

vec3 directLight = CalculateDirectLight();

vec3 indirectLight = CalculateIndirectLight();

// Material properties

vec3 albedo = GetAlbedo();

float roughness = GetRoughness();

float metallic = GetMetallic();

// BRDF calculations

vec3 reflectedLight = CookTorranceBRDF(albedo, roughness,
metallic, directLight, indirectLight);

// Final color

gl_FragColor = vec4(reflectedLight, 1.0);

}
```

2. Material System

Implement a flexible material system that allows artists and designers to define PBR materials for objects in the game. This system should support texture maps for albedo, roughness, metallic, normal, and other PBR parameters. Consider adopting industry-standard texture formats, such as Albedo-AO-Roughness-Metallic (AARM) maps.

3. Lighting Model

Choose and implement a lighting model suitable for PBR. The most common model is the Cook-Torrance model, which accurately simulates microfacet-based reflections and is compatible with both metallic-roughness and specular-glossiness workflows.

4. HDR Rendering

PBR relies on high-dynamic-range (HDR) rendering to accurately capture the full range of lighting intensities. Ensure your game engine supports HDR rendering pipelines and tone mapping techniques to display HDR content on standard displays.

5. Environment Maps

Integrate environment maps (cubemaps or spherical harmonics) for IBL. These maps provide global illumination and accurate reflections. Consider using real-time or precomputed radiance transfer techniques to efficiently handle dynamic lighting changes.

6. Shadowing Techniques

Implement robust shadowing techniques, such as shadow mapping or ray tracing, to accurately simulate shadows in PBR-rendered scenes. Shadows significantly contribute to the realism of the visuals.

7. Art Pipeline

Develop an art pipeline that allows artists to create PBR-ready assets. This includes providing guidelines for texture map creation, material authoring, and asset exporting.

8. Real-time Updates

PBR should support real-time updates of materials and lighting. Implement techniques like texture streaming and hot-reloading of shaders and materials to enable quick iterations during game development.

9. Performance Optimization

Optimize PBR rendering for real-time performance. This may involve techniques like level-of-detail (LOD) for materials, culling, and using efficient rendering APIs like Vulkan or DirectX 12.

10. Documentation and Training

Provide thorough documentation and training materials for your team, including artists, designers, and engineers. PBR is a specialized field, and understanding its principles is crucial for achieving high-quality results.

Conclusion

Integrating PBR into a game engine elevates the visual fidelity of games and simulations. However, it's a complex process that requires expertise in rendering, shader development, and art asset creation. By following these steps and considering the mentioned aspects, you can successfully bring PBR to your game engine and create visually stunning and realistic virtual worlds.

Chapter 12: Environmental Techniques

Section 12.1: Procedural Terrain Generation

Procedural terrain generation is a fundamental technique for creating vast and realistic landscapes in games and simulations. Instead of manually designing every aspect of the terrain, you can use algorithms to generate terrain based on certain rules and parameters. This section explores the principles and methods of procedural terrain generation.

Benefits of Procedural Terrain Generation

Procedural terrain generation offers several advantages:

1. **Variety**: You can create diverse landscapes with different features, such as mountains, valleys, hills, and plains, without the need for extensive manual design.
2. **Efficiency**: Procedural generation can create large terrains efficiently, saving both time and memory compared to manually crafted terrains.
3. **Dynamic Worlds**: Terrain can adapt to changes in the game world, such as erosion, earthquakes, or player interactions.
4. **Infinite Worlds**: With procedural generation, you can potentially create infinite worlds, as terrain can be generated on-the-fly as the player explores.

Perlin Noise

Perlin noise is a widely used basis for procedural terrain generation. It is a gradient noise function that generates smooth, coherent noise patterns. These patterns can be interpreted to create various terrain features. Perlin noise is characterized by its ability to create natural-looking, organic shapes.

Here's a simplified example of generating 2D Perlin noise in Python:

```python
import noise

def generate_2d_noise(width, height, scale, octaves, persistence, lacunarity, seed):

world = [[0] * height for _ in range(width)]

for x in range(width):

for y in range(height):

amplitude = 1

frequency = 1

noise_height = 0

for _ in range(octaves):

sample_x = x / scale * frequency

sample_y = y / scale * frequency

perlin_value = noise.snoise2(sample_x + seed, sample_y + seed)

noise_height += perlin_value * amplitude

amplitude *= persistence

frequency *= lacunarity

world[x][y] = noise_height

return world
```

Terrain Features

To create terrain features like mountains, valleys, and rivers, you can apply various algorithms to the generated Perlin noise. For example, you can set thresholds to determine where mountains and valleys should be located, or you can simulate erosion processes to carve out riverbeds.

Realism and Artistic Control

Procedural terrain generation strikes a balance between realism and artistic control. You can adjust parameters like the scale, octaves, persistence, and lacunarity to achieve the desired level of detail and style for your game's terrain. Additionally, you can blend procedural generation with manually designed elements to create truly unique landscapes.

Conclusion

Procedural terrain generation is a valuable technique for creating expansive and dynamic virtual worlds. By understanding and implementing algorithms like Perlin noise, you can generate diverse terrains that enhance the immersive quality of your game or simulation. This technique is a powerful tool in the game developer's toolkit, offering flexibility and efficiency in terrain design.

Section 12.2: Dynamic Weather Systems

Dynamic weather systems add realism and immersion to games and simulations by simulating changes in weather conditions over time. These systems can affect gameplay, visuals, and even audio. In this section, we'll explore the components and principles of dynamic weather systems.

Components of a Dynamic Weather System

A dynamic weather system typically consists of the following components:

1. **Weather States**: Different weather states, such as clear skies, rain, snow, fog, and storms, are defined. Each state has associated properties like precipitation intensity, wind speed, and visibility.
2. **Transition Logic**: Rules or algorithms determine how and when weather transitions occur. Transitions can be gradual or sudden, depending on the desired effect.
3. **Visual Effects**: Weather states are visually represented in the game world. Raindrops, snowflakes, fog, and other visual effects are rendered to match the current weather state.
4. **Audio Effects**: Soundscapes change to match the weather. Rainfall, thunder, wind, and other audio elements create a more immersive experience.
5. **Gameplay Effects**: Weather can influence gameplay. For example, rain might make surfaces slippery, affect vehicle handling, or impact visibility.

Implementing a Dynamic Weather System

Here's a simplified example of how you might implement a dynamic weather system in a game using Python and Pygame:

```python
import pygame
import random

# Define weather states and their properties
weather_states = {
```

```python
    "Clear": {"precipitation": 0, "wind_speed": 0, "visibility": 100},
    "Rain": {"precipitation": 1, "wind_speed": 2, "visibility": 70},
    "Snow": {"precipitation": 1, "wind_speed": 1, "visibility": 60},
    "Fog": {"precipitation": 0, "wind_speed": 1, "visibility": 40},
}

current_weather = "Clear"

def change_weather():
    global current_weather
    # Randomly select a new weather state
    new_weather = random.choice(list(weather_states.keys()))
    current_weather = new_weather

# Game loop
while True:
    for event in pygame.event.get():
        if event.type == pygame.QUIT:
            pygame.quit()
            sys.exit()

    # Update weather periodically
    if random.random() < 0.01:
        change_weather()
```

 # Render the game world based on the current weather

precipitation = weather_states[current_weather]["precipitation"]

wind_speed = weather_states[current_weather]["wind_speed"]

visibility = weather_states[current_weather]["visibility"]

 # Render visuals and play audio based on the weather state

 # Update gameplay effects based on weather (e.g., player movement)

In this example, we have defined weather states and their properties. The weather changes randomly, but you can implement more sophisticated transition logic based on in-game events or time of day.

Realism and Immersion

Dynamic weather systems contribute to realism and immersion in games. Players feel more connected to the game world when they see and experience changing weather conditions. These systems require careful balance and tuning to ensure that weather effects enhance the gameplay and overall experience.

Conclusion

Dynamic weather systems are a powerful tool for enhancing the realism and immersion of games and simulations. By implementing weather states, transition logic, visual and audio effects, and gameplay impacts, you can create a more engaging and dynamic virtual world that responds to changing weather conditions.

Section 12.3: Ocean and Water Rendering

Ocean and water rendering are critical elements in many games and simulations, especially those set in maritime or aquatic environments. Achieving realistic and visually appealing water surfaces can significantly enhance the overall quality of the virtual world. In this section, we'll explore the techniques and principles of ocean and water rendering.

Principles of Realistic Water Rendering

Realistic water rendering involves simulating various physical phenomena that contribute to the appearance of water. Key principles include:

1. **Reflection**: Water reflects the surrounding environment, including objects, terrain, and the sky. Implementing screen-space reflections (SSR) or cube maps can achieve convincing reflection effects.
2. **Refraction**: When light enters water, it bends, causing objects submerged in the water to appear distorted. This effect is known as refraction and can be achieved using shader techniques.
3. **Surface Waves**: Simulating surface waves is crucial for creating the appearance of dynamic water. Gerstner waves, FFT (Fast Fourier Transform) waves, or procedural techniques can be used to generate waves.
4. **Transparency**: Water is translucent, allowing light to penetrate its surface. Accurate transparency and subsurface scattering effects are essential for realistic water.
5. **Caustics**: Caustics are the patterns of light and shadow formed on underwater surfaces due to the distortion of light by waves. Implementing caustics can enhance the underwater environment.

Implementing Water Rendering

Here's a simplified example of water rendering using OpenGL and GLSL shaders:

// Vertex Shader

#version 330 core

layout(location = 0) in vec3 inPosition;

out vec3 fragPosition;

uniform mat4 projection;

uniform mat4 view;

uniform mat4 model;

void main()

{

gl_Position = projection * view * model * vec4(inPosition, 1.0);

fragPosition = vec3(model * vec4(inPosition, 1.0));

}

// Fragment Shader

#version 330 core

in vec3 fragPosition;

out vec4 FragColor;

uniform vec3 lightPos;

uniform vec3 viewPos;

```glsl
void main()

{

// Calculate reflection vector

vec3 viewDir = normalize(viewPos - fragPosition);

vec3 reflectDir = reflect(-viewDir, normalize(vec3(0.0, 1.0, 0.0)));

// Calculate fresnel term

float fresnel = max(dot(viewDir, reflectDir), 0.0);

fresnel = pow(fresnel, 2.0);

// Calculate final color (blend reflection and refraction)

vec3 reflectionColor = texture(reflectionTexture, reflectDir).rgb;

vec3 refractionColor = texture(refractionTexture, viewDir).rgb;

vec3 finalColor = mix(reflectionColor, refractionColor, fresnel);

FragColor = vec4(finalColor, 1.0);

}
```

This shader code combines reflection and refraction to simulate the appearance of water. It calculates reflection and refraction vectors, applies the Fresnel term, and blends the two colors.

Optimizations

Realistic water rendering can be computationally expensive. To optimize performance, techniques like level of detail (LOD), screen-space techniques, and impostors can be employed to reduce the rendering load. Additionally, using normal and displacement maps can enhance the appearance of water surfaces.

Conclusion

Ocean and water rendering are essential for creating immersive aquatic environments in games and simulations. By understanding the principles of reflection, refraction, surface waves, transparency, and caustics, and by implementing appropriate rendering techniques, developers can achieve visually stunning water effects that greatly enhance the player's experience.

Section 12.4: Interactive Vegetation and Foliage

Interactive vegetation and foliage play a crucial role in enhancing the realism and immersion of outdoor scenes in video games and simulations. This section delves into the techniques and considerations involved in implementing interactive vegetation and foliage systems.

Importance of Vegetation

In a virtual world, vegetation and foliage not only provide visual richness but also contribute to the overall atmosphere and gameplay. They create lush forests, vibrant meadows, and dense jungles, making the environment more believable. Additionally, interactive vegetation can affect gameplay by providing cover, affecting visibility, or acting as collectibles.

Techniques for Interactive Vegetation

1. Procedural Generation: Procedural techniques are often used to generate vast amounts of foliage efficiently. Algorithms like L-

systems or noise-based approaches can create various plant structures.

2. Wind Animation: To simulate the movement of leaves, branches, and grass in response to wind, vertex shaders can be employed to animate vegetation. Simple sine wave calculations applied to vertex positions can create convincing wind effects.

3. Collision Detection: Interactive vegetation should respond to player interactions and physics. Implementing collision detection allows players to interact with plants by pushing them, walking through them, or collecting them.

4. Level of Detail (LOD): Foliage can be computationally expensive, especially in open-world games. LOD techniques can be used to simplify the geometry and reduce rendering costs as the player moves farther away from the foliage.

5. Dynamic Instancing: For dense forests or fields of grass, dynamic instancing techniques can optimize rendering by drawing multiple instances of the same vegetation model in a single draw call.

Shader Effects for Vegetation

1. Translucency: Leaves and foliage are typically translucent. Achieving realistic translucency in shaders is essential to mimic the way light scatters through leaves and creates a soft, natural look.

2. Shadowing: Foliage should cast shadows on the ground and other objects. Shadow maps and techniques like Percentage-Closer Soft Shadows (PCSS) can help achieve convincing shadow effects.

3. Subsurface Scattering (SSS): Some vegetation, especially thin leaves, benefits from SSS effects to realistically simulate light penetration and scattering within the plant material.

Interactive Elements

1. Growth and Destruction: Interactive vegetation systems can implement growth and destruction mechanics. For instance, plants may grow or wither over time, or players can chop down trees or destroy bushes.

2. Collectibles and Crafting: Foliage can be a source of resources for crafting or power-ups. Collecting plants for healing or building items adds depth to gameplay.

Optimization and Performance

Efficient rendering of interactive vegetation requires careful optimization. Techniques like culling (frustum and occlusion), LOD management, and batching are essential to maintain good performance, especially in densely vegetated areas.

Conclusion

Interactive vegetation and foliage contribute significantly to the visual appeal and gameplay of outdoor environments in video games and simulations. By employing procedural generation, wind animation, collision detection, shader effects, and interactive elements, developers can create lush and engaging virtual worlds that captivate players and enhance the overall gaming experience.

Section 12.5: Realistic Sky and Atmospheric Rendering

Realistic sky and atmospheric rendering are crucial aspects of creating immersive outdoor environments in video games and simulations. This section explores the techniques and considerations involved in achieving convincing sky and atmospheric effects.

The Importance of Sky and Atmosphere

The sky and atmosphere provide the backdrop for outdoor scenes, setting the mood and enhancing the visual quality of the game world. Realistic sky and atmospheric rendering contribute to the overall atmosphere and can be instrumental in storytelling and gameplay.

Techniques for Realistic Sky and Atmosphere

1. Skybox and Skydome: The simplest approach is to use a skybox or skydome texture to simulate the sky. This approach is efficient and works well for many scenarios.

2. Dynamic Sky: For more realism, dynamic sky systems can be employed. These systems simulate the changing appearance of the sky and weather conditions over time. They often involve complex shaders and calculations to achieve effects like dynamic clouds, sunsets, and weather transitions.

3. Atmospheric Scattering: Atmospheric scattering models, such as Rayleigh and Mie scattering, simulate how sunlight interacts with air molecules and particles. This technique can produce the characteristic blue sky and reddish sunsets seen in the real world.

4. Day-Night Cycle: Implementing a day-night cycle adds depth to outdoor scenes. It involves changing the position and intensity of the sun and moon, altering lighting conditions, and affecting gameplay aspects like visibility and NPC behavior.

5. Weather Systems: Realistic weather systems can include rain, snow, fog, and storms. Weather effects can impact visibility, audio, and gameplay, making the world feel dynamic and alive.

Shader Effects for Sky and Atmosphere

1. Skybox Shaders: Shader effects for skyboxes may include simple scrolling cloud layers, the sun's position and glare, and transitions between day and night.

2. Volumetric Clouds: To create realistic clouds, volumetric cloud shaders simulate cloud formation, movement, and interaction with light. They can produce dynamic, realistic cloudscapes.

3. Light Scattering: Shaders for atmospheric scattering models are complex but essential for creating realistic skies. They involve calculations for Rayleigh and Mie scattering, which affect the sky's color and the appearance of the sun and moon.

Light Interaction

Realistic sky and atmosphere rendering should interact with in-game lighting. The color and intensity of sunlight should change based on the time of day and weather conditions, influencing the overall scene's lighting.

Performance Considerations

While achieving realism is crucial, it's equally important to maintain good performance. Complex shaders and calculations for dynamic skies and atmospheric scattering can be computationally expensive. To address this, techniques like level of detail (LOD) for the sky, efficient cloud rendering, and optimizations in the shader code should be implemented.

Conclusion

Realistic sky and atmospheric rendering are essential for creating immersive outdoor environments in games and simulations. By employing techniques like dynamic skies, atmospheric scattering, and weather systems, developers can transport players to dynamic and visually captivating virtual worlds. Careful consideration of performance optimizations ensures that these effects enhance, rather than detract from, the gaming experience.

Chapter 13: Sound Spatialization and Advanced Techniques

In this chapter, we explore sound spatialization and various advanced techniques to enhance the audio experience in video games and simulations. Sound is a vital component of immersive gameplay, and by utilizing spatialization and other techniques, developers can create more realistic and engaging auditory experiences.

Section 13.1: 3D Sound Systems

3D Sound: When designing a game or simulation, achieving realistic and immersive audio is just as important as impressive visuals. Sound plays a significant role in enhancing immersion and providing players with valuable feedback. In a 3D virtual environment, sound should not just be heard; it should also be perceived as coming from a specific location or direction. This concept is known as sound spatialization.

Spatialized Sound: In the real world, sounds come from various directions and distances. Our brains process these auditory cues to determine where sounds are coming from, allowing us to pinpoint their locations accurately. Spatialized sound in games and simulations attempts to recreate this experience by making sounds appear to come from specific positions in the virtual environment.

Importance of 3D Sound: 3D sound is crucial for creating a sense of presence and immersion. Without it, all sounds would appear to come from the same point, which can be disorienting and less engaging. For example, in a first-person shooter game, hearing an enemy's footsteps approaching from behind or the direction of gunfire can be vital for gameplay.

Basic Principles: To achieve 3D sound, developers need to consider several principles:

1. **Positional Audio**: Each sound source in the game world has a position. The player's position and orientation are also considered. Based on these factors, the game engine calculates how the sound should be heard by the player.
2. **Directionality**: Sounds should have directionality, which means that their volume and timbre change based on the listener's orientation relative to the sound source.
3. **Distance Attenuation**: As sound travels, it attenuates or becomes quieter. This attenuation should be realistic and depend on factors like distance, obstacles, and environmental conditions.
4. **Doppler Effect**: The Doppler effect simulates the change in pitch of a sound as it moves relative to the listener. For example, a car engine will sound different as it approaches and passes by.

Audio Technologies: Various audio technologies and techniques are used to achieve 3D sound:

1. **Binaural Audio**: This technique uses two microphones to capture sound as it enters the ears, simulating human hearing. When played back through headphones, it provides an immersive 3D audio experience.
2. **HRTF (Head-Related Transfer Function)**: HRTF is a mathematical model that describes how sound is altered as it enters the ears and interacts with the head and body. Implementing HRTF in audio processing can enhance spatialization.
3. **Sound Occlusion and Reflection**: Sounds should be occluded (muffled) when they pass through obstacles or

reflected when they bounce off surfaces. These effects are essential for creating realistic audio environments.

Game Engines and APIs: Many game engines and audio APIs provide built-in support for 3D sound and spatialization. Developers can utilize these tools to simplify the implementation of spatialized audio in their games and simulations.

Conclusion: 3D sound systems are a crucial component of immersive audio experiences in games and simulations. By simulating the way we hear sounds in the real world, developers can enhance immersion and provide players with valuable auditory cues, contributing to more engaging and realistic virtual worlds. In the next sections, we will explore advanced sound techniques, including reverb and reflections, to further enhance the audio experience.

Section 13.2: Reverberation and Reflections

In this section, we delve into the concepts of reverberation and reflections in audio engineering and their application in creating realistic sound environments in games and simulations. These audio effects are essential for providing depth and authenticity to the auditory experience, making virtual worlds feel more convincing.

Reverberation: Reverberation, often referred to as "reverb," is the persistence of sound in an environment after the sound source has stopped emitting. In the real world, when you clap your hands in a large, empty room, you can hear the sound bouncing off the walls, ceiling, and floor, gradually diminishing over time. This phenomenon adds a sense of space to the audio, allowing you to perceive the size and characteristics of the environment.

Simulating Reverberation: In game audio, simulating reverb involves modeling the acoustic properties of the virtual environment and calculating how sound reflections and absorption affect the audio. Game engines and audio middleware often provide tools and parameters to control reverb, allowing developers to define the characteristics of the virtual environment.

Convolution Reverb: One common technique for achieving realistic reverb is convolution reverb. This method involves capturing the impulse response of a real-world location or space, such as a cathedral or concert hall, by recording a short, sharp sound (an impulse) within that space. The impulse response recording contains information about how sound behaves in that environment, including reflections and decay over time.

Applying Convolution Reverb: To apply convolution reverb in a game or simulation, developers convolve the recorded impulse response with the audio signal. This process simulates how the sound would have reverberated if it had been played in the real-world location. The result is a highly realistic and immersive audio experience that matches the virtual environment's acoustics.

Reflections: While reverb deals with the persistence of sound in an environment, reflections focus on the directional bouncing of sound off surfaces. In the real world, if you shout in a canyon or near a large building, you can hear the echo as your voice bounces off the surfaces and returns to your ears.

Simulating Reflections: Simulating reflections involves calculating the paths of sound rays as they bounce off surfaces in the virtual environment. These calculations consider factors such as the distance between the source and the reflective surface, the angle of incidence, and the material properties of the surface. By accurately modeling sound reflections, developers can create a convincing sense of space and depth in the audio.

Real-Time Reflections: Real-time audio reflections can be computationally expensive, especially in complex scenes with many reflective surfaces. Game engines often use techniques like ray tracing or reflection probes to efficiently calculate and simulate audio reflections in real time.

Conclusion: Reverberation and reflections are fundamental to creating realistic and immersive audio experiences in games and simulations. These techniques add depth, authenticity, and a sense of space to the auditory environment, enhancing the overall immersion and making virtual worlds feel more convincing to the player. In the next sections, we will explore further advanced audio techniques, including sound propagation and environmental soundscapes.

Section 13.3: Sound Propagation

In this section, we delve into the fascinating world of sound propagation, which is a critical aspect of creating realistic audio environments in games and simulations. Sound propagation is all about simulating how sound travels through the virtual world, interacts with objects, and reaches the player's ears. Achieving accurate sound propagation enhances immersion and can significantly improve the overall gaming experience.

Basic Principles of Sound Propagation: Sound propagation involves simulating the movement of sound waves as they travel through the virtual environment. Several key principles come into play:

1. **Sound Speed**: Sound travels at different speeds through various materials (e.g., air, water, solids). Simulating these differences is crucial for realistic sound propagation.
2. **Sound Attenuation**: As sound waves travel through a

medium, they lose energy and become quieter. Factors like distance, obstacles, and material properties affect sound attenuation.

3. **Reflection and Diffraction**: Sound waves can reflect off surfaces, creating echoes and reverb. They can also diffract around obstacles, leading to complex sound interactions.

4. **Direct and Indirect Sound**: Players perceive both direct sound (reaching the ears directly from the source) and indirect sound (reaching the ears after multiple reflections). Balancing these elements is essential for immersion.

Ray Tracing for Sound Propagation: Ray tracing, a technique often associated with realistic graphics rendering, is also used for sound propagation. In this context, ray tracing involves simulating the paths of sound rays as they travel through the virtual environment. Each ray represents a possible sound path from the source to the listener.

Ray tracing for sound propagation allows for:

• **Realistic Reflections**: Sound rays accurately bounce off surfaces, creating echoes and reverb.

• **Obstacle Interactions**: Rays can diffract around obstacles, leading to realistic sound occlusion and diffraction effects.

• **Environmental Considerations**: Factors like temperature, humidity, and wind can affect sound speed and attenuation, adding complexity to the simulation.

Sound Propagation in Game Engines: Modern game engines often include sound propagation features. Developers can define the acoustic properties of materials and spaces within the environment, such as absorption coefficients and reflection patterns. The engine then uses this information to simulate sound propagation dynamically during gameplay.

Code Example:

```
// Pseudocode for simulating sound propagation with ray tracing

foreach (soundSource in level.soundSources) {

foreach (listener in level.listeners) {

// Calculate direct sound path

directSound          =          traceSoundRay(soundSource.position,
listener.position);

directSoundVolume = calculateAttenuation(directSound);

// Calculate indirect sound paths (reflections, diffractions)

foreach (reflectionSurface in level.reflectiveSurfaces) {

reflectedSound          =          traceSoundRay(soundSource.position,
reflectionSurface);

reflectedSoundVolume = calculateAttenuation(reflectedSound);

// Add reflected sound to the overall sound reaching the listener

listener.hearSound(reflectedSoundVolume);

}

// Combine direct and indirect sound contributions for this
source-listener pair
```

```
totalSoundVolume        =        directSoundVolume        +
sumOfReflectedSoundVolumes;

// Add the total sound to the listener's audio mix

listener.hearSound(totalSoundVolume);

    }

}
```

Conclusion: Sound propagation is a crucial component of creating immersive audio experiences in games and simulations. By simulating the movement of sound waves, including reflections and diffractions, developers can transport players into rich, believable virtual worlds where audio is an integral part of the experience. In the next section, we will explore realistic audio effects and techniques that enhance the overall soundscape.

Section 13.4: Realistic Audio Effects

In this section, we delve into the realm of realistic audio effects, which are essential for creating an immersive and believable auditory experience in games and simulations. Realistic audio effects go beyond simple playback of sound samples and encompass techniques that mimic how sound behaves in the real world, adding depth and authenticity to the audio environment.

Dynamic Range and Compression: One crucial aspect of realistic audio is simulating dynamic range. In the real world, sounds have varying volumes, from whisper-quiet to ear-piercingly loud. This dynamic range is crucial for immersion, as it allows players to distinguish between subtle sounds and loud, impactful ones. Implementing dynamic range in audio involves techniques such as dynamic range compression, which adjusts the loudness of sounds to fit within a specified range.

Convolution Reverb: Convolution reverb is a technique used to simulate realistic room acoustics. It involves capturing the acoustic characteristics of real spaces (e.g., concert halls, caves) and applying them to in-game sounds. When a sound is played, it is convolved with the room's impulse response, creating the illusion that the sound is occurring in that physical space. This adds a layer of authenticity to the audio environment.

Doppler Effect: The Doppler effect simulates the change in pitch (frequency) of a sound as an object emitting the sound approaches or moves away from the listener. In games, this effect is crucial for simulating moving objects like cars, planes, or projectiles. Implementing the Doppler effect requires adjusting the pitch of a sound based on the relative velocity of the source and the listener.

HRTF (Head-Related Transfer Function): HRTF is a technique used to simulate how sounds are filtered by the shape of the human ears and head before reaching the eardrums. This filtering affects the perceived direction and distance of sounds. By applying HRTF to audio sources, developers can create realistic 3D audio positioning, allowing players to accurately locate sounds in a virtual environment.

Environmental Audio Effects: To enhance realism, environmental audio effects can be applied. For example, underwater audio should sound muffled and distorted, while sounds in a forest might have subtle echoes due to the surrounding trees. These effects add depth and believability to the game world.

Code Example (Dynamic Range Compression):

// Pseudocode for dynamic range compression

```
foreach (audioSource in level.audioSources) {

// Capture audio sample

audioSample = audioSource.getSample();

// Apply dynamic range compression

compressedSample = applyCompression(audioSample, threshold,
ratio, makeupGain);

// Play the compressed sample

audioSource.play(compressedSample);

}
```

Conclusion: Realistic audio effects are essential for immersing players in the virtual worlds of games and simulations. By simulating dynamic range, using convolution reverb, incorporating the Doppler effect, applying HRTF, and utilizing environmental audio effects, developers can create audio experiences that are not only convincing but also enhance gameplay and storytelling. In the next section, we will explore the concept of environmental soundscapes, where audio plays a crucial role in defining the ambiance of a virtual world.

Section 13.5: Environmental Soundscapes

In the world of game audio, creating compelling environmental soundscapes is a crucial component of immersing players in the game's universe. Soundscapes are the sonic backdrop of a game environment, consisting of ambient sounds, background music, and environmental effects. In this section, we will explore the techniques and considerations for designing and implementing immersive environmental soundscapes.

Understanding the Environment: The first step in designing an environmental soundscape is understanding the virtual world's setting. Whether it's a bustling city, a tranquil forest, or a post-apocalyptic wasteland, the audio should reflect the atmosphere and context. Consider the time of day, weather conditions, and the presence of any unique elements like wildlife or machinery.

Layering Sounds: To create depth in soundscapes, audio designers use layering. Different layers of sounds are combined to form a cohesive auditory experience. For instance, in a forest soundscape, layers might include birdsong, rustling leaves, and distant waterfalls. Each layer contributes to the overall ambiance, and they can be dynamically controlled to adapt to in-game events.

Interactive Soundscapes: To enhance immersion, soundscapes should react to player actions and events. For example, as the player enters a dark cave, the environmental soundscape should shift to echoey, eerie sounds. When a player encounters a thunderstorm, the soundscape should adapt to intensify the storm's impact. Interactive soundscapes add a layer of realism and responsiveness to the game world.

Audio Triggers and Emitters: To synchronize sounds with in-game events or objects, audio triggers and emitters are used. Triggers are events that activate specific sounds, while emitters are virtual sound sources that emit audio into the game world. For example, a creaking door sound is triggered when the player interacts with a door object. Emitters can be attached to moving objects, such as vehicles, to create realistic sound movement.

Music and Stingers: Background music and stingers (short musical cues) play a significant role in setting the game's tone and highlighting key moments. Transitioning between different musical themes can signal changes in gameplay or narrative, while stingers can punctuate important events.

Code Example (Audio Trigger):

// Pseudocode for an audio trigger when a player enters a cave

```
function onPlayerEnterCave() {

caveAmbience.play();

caveAmbience.setVolume(0.8);

caveAmbience.setReverb("cave");

}
```

Conclusion: Environmental soundscapes are a powerful tool for enhancing immersion and storytelling in games and simulations. By carefully designing and implementing soundscapes that match the virtual environment's context, using layering and interactivity, and leveraging audio triggers and emitters, developers can create audio experiences that complement the visual elements and provide players with a truly immersive adventure. In the next chapter, we will explore networking and multiplayer advanced topics, focusing on the intricacies of creating multiplayer game experiences.

Chapter 14: Networking and Multiplayer Advanced Topics

Section 14.1: Multiplayer Game Architectures

Multiplayer gaming has evolved significantly over the years, from local split-screen experiences to massive online worlds. Building effective multiplayer game architectures is crucial for creating engaging and seamless multiplayer experiences. In this section, we will delve into various multiplayer game architectures and their considerations.

Client-Server Architecture: The most common multiplayer architecture is the client-server model. In this setup, one player acts as the server, hosting the game world and managing game logic, while other players (clients) connect to the server to participate. This architecture provides centralized control, making it easier to implement game rules and prevent cheating.

Peer-to-Peer (P2P) Architecture: In a P2P architecture, each player's device acts as both a client and a server, communicating directly with other players. P2P architectures are suitable for games with small player counts and limited complexity. They are often used in local multiplayer or for games that do not require a dedicated server.

Hybrid Architectures: Some multiplayer games use hybrid architectures that combine elements of both client-server and P2P models. For example, a client-server architecture might be used for game setup and management, while P2P connections handle in-game communication between players.

Considerations for Client-Server: - **Scalability**: Client-server architectures require robust servers to handle player connections. Scalability and load balancing are critical considerations. - **Latency**: Minimizing latency is essential for a smooth player experience. Server location and efficient data transfer protocols are factors to consider. - **Authority**: The server often has the final say on game state, which can lead to issues like lag compensation for fast-paced games.

Considerations for P2P: - **Synchronization**: P2P architectures must ensure all players have synchronized game state. Time synchronization and reconciliation are crucial. - **Cheating**: P2P architectures can be susceptible to cheating, as players have more control. Anti-cheat mechanisms are necessary. - **Connectivity**: P2P requires direct connections between players, which can be challenging in situations with firewalls or NAT traversal issues.

Code Example (Client-Server Connection):

```
# Pseudocode for a client connecting to a multiplayer server

serverAddress = "192.168.1.100"

port = 8000

client = new Client()

client.connect(serverAddress, port)
```

Conclusion: Choosing the right multiplayer game architecture depends on the game's scale, complexity, and requirements. Client-server architectures provide centralized control and are suitable for most online multiplayer games, while P2P architectures work well for smaller-scale, local multiplayer experiences. Hybrid approaches can offer flexibility in certain scenarios. In the next section, we will explore real-time data synchronization in multiplayer games.

Section 14.2: Real-time Data Synchronization

Real-time data synchronization is a fundamental aspect of multiplayer game development. It ensures that all players in a game world share the same game state, allowing for a consistent and fair multiplayer experience. In this section, we'll explore the key concepts and techniques involved in real-time data synchronization.

The Challenge of Synchronization

In a multiplayer game, players may be geographically dispersed and playing on devices with varying processing power and network conditions. Synchronizing game data across all clients and the server in real-time while accommodating these differences can be challenging.

Key Synchronization Concepts

1. State Replication

State replication involves sending updates about game objects' states (e.g., player positions, health, or scores) to all connected clients. These updates are sent at regular intervals to maintain consistency. For example, if a player moves, their new position must be synchronized with all other players.

2. Delta Compression

Delta compression is a technique that reduces the amount of data sent over the network by only transmitting the changes (delta) between the previous and current states. This optimization helps minimize bandwidth usage and reduces latency.

3. Client Prediction

Client prediction allows players to perform actions locally (e.g., moving their character) and then immediately see the results without waiting for confirmation from the server. The server later validates these actions, and if necessary, adjusts the game state to ensure fairness.

Techniques for Real-time Synchronization

1. Reliable vs. Unreliable Messages

Network messages can be categorized as reliable (guaranteed delivery) or unreliable (may be lost). Reliable messages are crucial for important game events, while unreliable messages are suitable for non-essential updates, such as character animations.

2. Dead Reckoning

Dead reckoning is a prediction technique used to extrapolate the positions of moving objects based on their last known state and velocity. This can reduce the need for frequent updates and save bandwidth.

3. Lag Compensation

Lag compensation techniques aim to mitigate the effects of network latency. Techniques like client-side prediction and server reconciliation help ensure that actions taken by players are fair, even when there is a delay between input and its effect on the game world.

Code Example (State Replication):

 # Pseudocode for replicating player position

class Player:

def __init__(self):

self.position = Vector3(0, 0, 0)

def update_position(self, new_position):

self.position = new_position

 # Send position update to other clients

network.send_position_update(self, new_position)

Conclusion

Real-time data synchronization is a critical aspect of multiplayer game development, enabling players to have a shared and consistent gaming experience. It involves replicating game state, optimizing data transmission, and implementing techniques like client prediction and lag compensation. Careful consideration of synchronization mechanisms is essential for creating engaging and responsive multiplayer games. In the next section, we'll explore networking topologies and protocols used in multiplayer games.

Section 14.3: Networking Topologies and Protocols

In the realm of multiplayer game development, selecting the appropriate networking topology and protocol is crucial for ensuring efficient communication and a smooth gaming experience. In this section, we'll delve into various networking topologies and protocols commonly used in multiplayer games.

Networking Topologies

1. Peer-to-Peer (P2P)

Peer-to-peer networking is a decentralized approach where each player's device communicates directly with other players. P2P is suitable for games with a small number of participants and minimal server involvement. It's often used in games like Minecraft and some peer-hosted online shooters.

Pros: - Low server maintenance. - Reduced latency for peer-to-peer interactions.

Cons: - Limited scalability. - Susceptible to cheating and synchronization challenges.

2. Client-Server

Client-server is a centralized model where a dedicated server manages the game state and serves as an intermediary for all clients. This topology is common in most online multiplayer games, especially those with larger player bases.

Pros: - Centralized control ensures consistency. - Scalability for a large number of players. - Easier anti-cheat measures.

Cons: - Requires server infrastructure and maintenance. - Increased latency due to server-client communication.

3. Hybrid

Hybrid topologies combine elements of both peer-to-peer and client-server models. They are often used in games that want to leverage the strengths of both approaches. For example, a game might use P2P for low-latency interactions within a local region and switch to a server-based model for broader, cross-region play.

Networking Protocols

1. UDP (User Datagram Protocol)

UDP is a connectionless, low-latency protocol favored for real-time applications like online gaming. It provides fast data transmission but lacks built-in reliability, requiring game developers to implement their own error handling and message sequencing.

2. TCP (Transmission Control Protocol)

TCP is a connection-oriented protocol known for its reliability. It ensures that data arrives intact and in the correct order. While this is beneficial for certain aspects of multiplayer gaming (e.g., chat or updates), it can introduce latency due to its acknowledgment mechanism.

Code Example (UDP vs. TCP):

 # Pseudocode for sending a message over UDP

udp_socket.sendto(message, (remote_ip, remote_port))

 # Pseudocode for sending a message over TCP

tcp_socket.connect((server_ip, server_port))

tcp_socket.send(message)

Conclusion

Choosing the right networking topology and protocol is a critical decision in multiplayer game development. Peer-to-peer, client-server, and hybrid topologies each have their strengths and weaknesses, depending on the game's requirements. Similarly, UDP and TCP protocols offer different trade-offs in terms of speed and reliability. Game developers must carefully consider their choices to create a multiplayer experience that is both responsive and robust. In the next section, we'll explore security and anti-cheat measures in the context of multiplayer games.

Section 14.4: Security and Anti-cheat Measures

Ensuring the security and fairness of online multiplayer games is of paramount importance. In this section, we'll explore various security and anti-cheat measures that game developers can implement to protect their games from cheating, hacking, and unauthorized access.

Security Measures

1. Authentication and Authorization

Implement robust authentication mechanisms to verify the identity of players during login. Use secure protocols like OAuth or OpenID

Connect. After authentication, employ authorization to determine what actions each player is allowed to perform in the game.

2. Encryption

Encrypt communication between clients and servers using strong encryption algorithms like TLS/SSL. This prevents eavesdropping and man-in-the-middle attacks, ensuring data confidentiality and integrity.

3. Input Validation

Thoroughly validate player inputs on both clients and servers to prevent malicious data from being injected. Input validation helps thwart attacks such as SQL injection and cross-site scripting (XSS).

4. Server-Side Validation

Never rely solely on client-side validation. Always validate important actions and decisions on the server. This prevents clients from manipulating game mechanics.

Anti-cheat Measures

1. Server Authority

In a client-server architecture, let the server be the authority on critical game mechanics. For instance, if a player claims to have dealt massive damage, the server should validate this before accepting it.

2. Cheat Detection Algorithms

Implement cheat detection algorithms that analyze player behavior and statistics. Unusual or impossible actions (e.g., instant kills or impossibly high scores) can trigger automatic flagging for investigation.

3. Regular Updates

Frequently update your game to fix vulnerabilities and exploits. Cheaters often reverse-engineer games to find weaknesses, so staying ahead is crucial.

4. Ban Systems

Create a system for banning cheaters. Track their activities and apply temporary or permanent bans as necessary. However, be cautious and avoid false positives.

Code Example (Authentication):

```
# Pseudocode for user authentication

if user_exists(username):

stored_hashed_password = get_password_hash(username)

if verify_password(input_password, stored_hashed_password):

generate_and_return_jwt_token(username)

else:

return_error("Invalid username or password")
```

Conclusion

Maintaining the security and integrity of a multiplayer game is an ongoing process. Developers must continuously adapt to new cheating techniques and security threats. By implementing strong authentication, encryption, input validation, and server-side validation, as well as employing cheat detection algorithms and ban systems, developers can create a fair and secure gaming environment that enhances the player experience. In the next section, we'll explore scalable multiplayer systems to accommodate a growing player base.

Section 14.5: Scalable Multiplayer Systems

As your multiplayer game gains popularity, the demands on your infrastructure grow. Scalability becomes crucial to accommodate a large and ever-increasing player base. In this section, we'll explore strategies and techniques for creating scalable multiplayer systems.

Load Balancing

Load balancing is a fundamental aspect of scalability. It involves distributing player connections and game server instances across multiple servers to ensure even resource usage and prevent overload. There are several load balancing strategies:

1. Round Robin

A simple approach where incoming connections are distributed sequentially to different servers in a circular order. While easy to implement, it may not account for variations in server load.

2. Least Connections

Servers with the fewest active connections receive new connections first. This strategy helps balance the load more effectively.

3. Weighted Round Robin

Assign weights to servers based on their capacity. Servers with higher weights receive more connections. This is useful when servers have varying capabilities.

4. Session Persistence

Ensure that all requests from a particular player are routed to the same server throughout their session. This is critical for maintaining game state consistency.

Database Scaling

As your player base grows, database performance becomes a bottleneck. Consider the following database scaling strategies:

1. Vertical Scaling

Increase the capacity of a single database server by upgrading hardware, such as CPU and RAM. This approach has limits and can be expensive.

2. Horizontal Scaling (Sharding)

Distribute data across multiple database servers, each responsible for a subset of data (shard). Sharding can significantly increase database capacity but requires careful data partitioning.

3. Caching

Implement caching mechanisms to reduce the load on the database. Use in-memory caching solutions like Redis or Memcached for frequently accessed data.

State Management

In multiplayer games, maintaining game state across multiple servers can be challenging. Consider these techniques:

1. Distributed Game State

Implement a distributed game state management system that synchronizes state changes across all servers in real-time.

2. Stateless Servers

Design servers to be stateless whenever possible. Keep critical game state centralized and replicate only what's necessary.

Auto-scaling

Leverage cloud infrastructure to automatically scale your game servers based on demand. Services like AWS Auto Scaling and Kubernetes can automatically add or remove servers as player activity fluctuates.

Code Example (Auto-scaling):

```
# Pseudocode for auto-scaling based on CPU usage

if cpu_usage > threshold:
```

```
scale_out()
```

elif cpu_usage < threshold:

```
scale_in()
```

Conclusion

Creating a scalable multiplayer system is essential for accommodating a growing player base and ensuring a smooth gaming experience. Load balancing, database scaling, effective state management, and auto-scaling are key components of a scalable architecture. By implementing these strategies, you can handle increased player traffic, maintain game performance, and deliver a high-quality multiplayer gaming experience. In the next chapter, we'll explore the intricacies of artificial intelligence (AI) and pathfinding in game development.

Chapter 15: AI and Pathfinding

Section 15.1: Basics of Game AI

Game Artificial Intelligence (AI) is an essential component for creating engaging and challenging gameplay experiences. It allows non-player characters (NPCs) and entities within a game to exhibit human-like behavior, make decisions, and respond dynamically to player actions. In this section, we'll delve into the basics of Game AI, including its core principles, common techniques, and how to implement AI in your games.

Understanding Game AI

Game AI aims to simulate intelligent behavior in computer-controlled entities, making them appear as if they are thinking and reacting autonomously. This AI is responsible for various aspects of gameplay, such as enemy behavior, character movements, decision-making, and pathfinding.

Core Principles of Game AI

1. **Perception:** AI entities need to perceive the game world to make informed decisions. This involves sensing the environment, detecting nearby objects and players, and gathering relevant information.
2. **Decision-Making:** Once the AI has perceived the world, it must decide what action to take. Decision-making algorithms range from simple rule-based systems to complex machine learning models.
3. **Behavior Trees:** Behavior trees are a common representation for AI decision-making. They consist of

nodes that define actions or conditions, arranged in a hierarchical structure. The AI evaluates these nodes to determine its behavior.

4. **State Machines:** State machines are another way to model AI behavior. They define a set of states and transitions between them, where each state represents a specific behavior or action.

5. **Pathfinding:** Pathfinding algorithms are crucial for AI-controlled entities to navigate the game world. These algorithms compute the best path from the AI's current location to its destination while avoiding obstacles.

Implementing Simple AI

Let's look at a basic example of implementing AI in a game. Suppose you have a game where an enemy character needs to follow and attack the player.

```python
class Enemy:

def __init__(self):

self.health = 100

self.damage = 10

self.speed = 5

self.target = None # The player

def follow_player(self):

if self.target:

# Calculate direction to the player

direction = self.target.position - self.position
```

```
direction.normalize()

# Move towards the player

self.position += direction * self.speed

def attack_player(self):

if self.target:

# Check if the player is within attack range

distance = self.position.distance_to(self.target.position)

if distance < self.attack_range:

self.target.take_damage(self.damage)
```

In this example, the Enemy class has methods to follow and attack the player. It calculates the direction to the player, moves toward them, and checks if the player is within attack range.

Conclusion

Game AI is a vast and exciting field, and this section provides a foundation for understanding its core principles and basic implementation. As you explore more advanced topics in AI, you can create increasingly sophisticated and challenging AI behaviors in your games.

In the following sections of this chapter, we will delve into more advanced AI techniques, including decision trees, pathfinding, and machine learning in game AI.

Section 15.2: Decision Trees and Finite State Machines

In the realm of game AI, Decision Trees and Finite State Machines (FSMs) are two fundamental techniques for modeling and controlling the behavior of non-player characters (NPCs) and entities. These methods provide structured approaches to decision-making and state transitions, enabling AI to respond dynamically to changing game conditions. In this section, we'll explore Decision Trees and FSMs, their principles, and how to use them in game development.

Decision Trees

A Decision Tree is a hierarchical model used to make decisions based on input conditions. It consists of nodes representing conditions or actions and branches that connect these nodes. Decision Trees are well-suited for representing complex decision-making processes in games.

Anatomy of a Decision Tree

- **Root Node:** The starting point of the tree.

- **Internal Nodes:** Nodes representing conditions or decisions.

- **Leaf Nodes:** Nodes representing actions or outcomes.

- **Branches:** Connections between nodes, indicating the flow of decisions.

Example of a Decision Tree

Consider a scenario where an AI-controlled character needs to decide its next action based on the player's proximity and its health:

Root

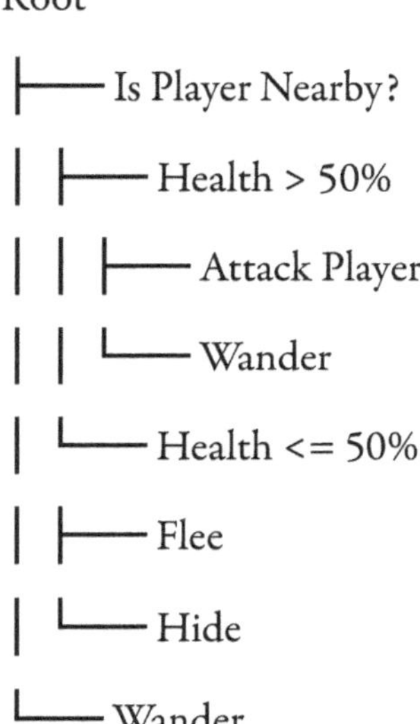

In this example, the Decision Tree starts at the root, checks if the player is nearby, and then considers the character's health to determine its action.

Finite State Machines (FSMs)

A Finite State Machine is a computational model used to represent an entity's behavior as a set of discrete states and transitions between them. FSMs are particularly useful for characters or entities with well-defined behavior patterns.

Key Components of an FSM

- **States:** Discrete behaviors or conditions the entity can be in.

- **Transitions:** Conditions or triggers that cause the entity to switch between states.

- **Actions:** Actions or behaviors associated with each state.

Example of an FSM

Let's consider a simple FSM for an NPC character with three states: "Idle," "Patrol," and "Chase." The transitions between states are triggered by specific conditions:

Idle -—(Player Spotted)—-> Chase

Chase -—(Player Lost)——> Patrol

Patrol -—(Player Spotted)—-> Chase

In this FSM, the NPC starts in the "Idle" state, transitions to "Chase" when it spots the player, and switches to "Patrol" when it loses sight of the player.

Implementing Decision Trees and FSMs

Implementing Decision Trees and FSMs in code involves defining the structure, conditions, and actions associated with each node or state. These structures can be handcrafted or learned from data using machine learning techniques.

In summary, Decision Trees and Finite State Machines are valuable tools for modeling game AI behavior. Decision Trees provide a hierarchical approach to decision-making, while FSMs are ideal for representing behaviors with distinct states and transitions. Game developers can choose the technique that best suits their AI requirements and design AI systems that enhance gameplay and immersion.

Section 15.3: Navigation Meshes and Pathfinding

In game development, character movement and pathfinding are crucial aspects of creating engaging and believable worlds. Navigation meshes (nav meshes) and pathfinding algorithms play a pivotal role in determining how characters, whether controlled by players or AI, navigate through complex environments. This section explores navigation meshes and various pathfinding techniques commonly used in game development.

Navigation Meshes (Nav Mesh)

A navigation mesh, often referred to as a nav mesh, is a data structure used to represent the walkable areas of a game's environment. It consists of a collection of convex polygons that define where characters can move. Nav meshes are used to efficiently calculate paths and avoid obstacles, making them an essential component of modern game AI.

Key Features of Nav Meshes

- **Polygon Representation:** Each polygon in the nav mesh represents a walkable area, and polygons are connected to form a coherent mesh.

- **Obstacle Avoidance:** Nav meshes allow characters to avoid obstacles by planning paths around them.

- **Efficiency:** They enable efficient pathfinding calculations, especially in complex 3D environments.

Pathfinding Algorithms

Pathfinding is the process of finding an optimal or near-optimal path from one location to another while avoiding obstacles and adhering to movement constraints. Several pathfinding algorithms are commonly used in games, including:

1. A* (A Star)

A* is a widely used pathfinding algorithm known for its efficiency and ability to find the shortest path. It employs a heuristic to prioritize nodes for exploration, making it suitable for a variety of game environments.

2. Dijkstra's Algorithm

Dijkstra's algorithm finds the shortest path in a graph by exploring all possible paths from the start node. While not as efficient as A* for games, it guarantees the shortest path.

3. Breadth-First Search (BFS)

BFS explores nodes in layers, starting from the source node and moving outward. It is efficient for finding the shortest path in unweighted graphs.

4. Depth-First Search (DFS)

DFS explores paths as deeply as possible before backtracking. While not suitable for finding the shortest path, it can be useful for other types of traversal.

5. Recast and Detour

Recast and Detour are popular libraries for navigation mesh generation and pathfinding. They are often used in conjunction with nav meshes to create efficient pathfinding solutions.

Implementing Pathfinding with Nav Meshes

To implement pathfinding with nav meshes, game developers typically follow these steps:

1. **Nav Mesh Generation:** Create or generate a navigation mesh that accurately represents the walkable areas of the game world. This step can be manual or automated, depending on the game's requirements.
2. **Pathfinding Initialization:** Set up pathfinding data structures and initialize them with the navigation mesh.
3. **Pathfinding Queries:** When a character needs to find a path from one location to another, initiate a pathfinding query using an algorithm like A*.
4. **Path Following:** Once a path is obtained, characters can follow it by moving from one polygon to another, avoiding obstacles and making decisions based on the path.
5. **Dynamic Obstacle Handling:** Handle dynamic obstacles and updates to the navigation mesh, ensuring that characters can adapt to changing environments.

In conclusion, navigation meshes and pathfinding algorithms are essential components of game AI and character movement. Nav meshes provide efficient representations of walkable areas, while pathfinding algorithms help characters navigate through complex environments, making games more immersive and interactive. Game developers should choose the right combination of techniques to suit their specific gameplay and performance needs.

Section 15.4: Dynamic Crowd Simulation

Dynamic crowd simulation is a critical aspect of modern video games, especially those aiming to create bustling and realistic virtual worlds. This section explores the challenges and techniques involved in simulating dynamic crowds within game environments.

Challenges in Dynamic Crowd Simulation

Simulating dynamic crowds in games presents several challenges that need to be addressed for a realistic and immersive experience:

1. Realistic Movement:

- **Pathfinding and Collision Avoidance:** Crowd members must navigate through complex environments while avoiding collisions with each other and static obstacles.

- **Variety in Movement:** Creating diverse movement patterns for crowd members to avoid the appearance of uniformity.

2. Scalability:

- **Handling Large Crowds:** Games may require the simulation of hundreds or even thousands of characters within a crowd. Efficient algorithms and data structures are needed to manage such scalability.

3. Behavior Modeling:

- **Emergent Behavior:** Crowd behavior should emerge from individual character decisions. Factors like group cohesion, panic, and leadership roles can influence the overall crowd behavior.

- **Realistic Reactions:** Characters in the crowd should react to changes in their environment, such as reacting to an emergency or reacting differently to stimuli.

4. Realistic Animation:

- **Animation Variety:** Creating diverse animations for crowd members to avoid repetitive motions.

- **Blending and Transitions:** Smoothly transitioning between animations to achieve natural movement.

Techniques for Dynamic Crowd Simulation

To address these challenges, game developers employ various techniques for dynamic crowd simulation:

1. Steering Behaviors:

- **Flocking Algorithms:** Flocking algorithms like Reynolds' Boids simulate behaviors like cohesion, separation, and alignment, resulting in realistic crowd movement.

- **Steering Behaviors:** Characters use steering behaviors like seek, flee, and evade to navigate through crowds and avoid obstacles.

2. Nav Meshes and Pathfinding:

- **Navigation Meshes:** Using navigation meshes for efficient pathfinding and collision avoidance in complex environments.

- **Hierarchical Pathfinding:** Employing hierarchical pathfinding to speed up calculations for large crowds.

3. Behavior Trees:

- **Behavior Trees:** Using behavior trees to model complex character behaviors and decision-making processes within the crowd.

4. Animation:

- **Motion Capture:** Incorporating motion-captured animations for realistic character movement.

- **Procedural Animation:** Combining pre-captured animations with procedural animation techniques to achieve a wide range of character motions.

5. Crowd Manager:

- **Crowd Manager:** Implementing a crowd manager that oversees the simulation of the entire crowd, handling updates, and interactions.

6. Level of Detail (LOD):

- **LOD Techniques:** Employing LOD techniques to reduce the complexity of distant crowd members to improve performance.

7. Reaction Systems:

- **Reaction Systems:** Implementing systems that enable characters to react realistically to events and changes in the environment.

Case Study: Riot and Panic Simulation

In some games, crowd simulations involve scenarios where crowds may react with panic or riot behavior. These situations require additional considerations, including factors that trigger panic, communication between characters, and crowd dynamics during a riot.

Dynamic crowd simulation is a multidisciplinary field that combines aspects of AI, animation, and game design. Implementing realistic crowd behavior enhances the overall immersion of a game world, making it feel vibrant and alive. Game developers must carefully balance performance and realism to create compelling crowd simulations tailored to their specific game scenarios and hardware constraints.

Section 15.5: Machine Learning in Game AI

Machine learning (ML) has revolutionized various fields, including the gaming industry. This section explores how machine learning techniques are used in game AI to create more intelligent and adaptive non-player characters (NPCs) and enhance overall gameplay experiences.

Leveraging Machine Learning in Game AI

1. Behavior Prediction:

- Machine learning models can be trained to predict player behavior. This is particularly useful in adaptive difficulty systems, where the game's challenge level adjusts based on the player's skill and behavior.

- Reinforcement learning can be used to train NPCs to learn from player actions and adapt their strategies accordingly.

2. Adaptive NPCs:

- ML models enable NPCs to adapt their behavior to changing game conditions. For example, in a real-time strategy (RTS) game, NPCs can use ML to optimize resource management, troop deployment, and decision-making.

- NPCs can learn from their mistakes and improve over time, providing a more engaging and challenging experience for players.

3. Natural Language Processing (NLP):

- NLP techniques can be used to enable NPCs to understand and respond to player-written or spoken dialogue. This is common in role-playing games (RPGs) and interactive storytelling games.

- Chatbots and virtual assistants within games can provide players with information and assistance using NLP.

4. Character Animation:

- ML-based animation systems can create more realistic and expressive character animations. For example, character facial expressions and body language can be generated based on in-game events and dialogue.

- Generative adversarial networks (GANs) can be used to create high-quality character animations and textures.

5. Player Behavior Analysis:

- ML algorithms can analyze player behavior to provide personalized experiences. For instance, in open-world games, NPCs can be generated or adapted to match a player's playstyle.

- Anomaly detection can be used to identify cheating or suspicious behavior in multiplayer games.

6. Procedural Content Generation:

- ML can assist in procedural content generation, creating dynamic and varied game worlds. This includes generating terrain, levels, textures, and even narrative elements.

- Generative models, such as variational autoencoders (VAEs), can be employed to create content that matches the desired style and theme.

7. Testing and Quality Assurance:

- Machine learning can automate testing processes by identifying bugs, glitches, or balance issues in the game. This accelerates the debugging and quality assurance phases of game development.

- ML-driven automated testing can simulate thousands of player interactions and scenarios to ensure game stability.

Case Study: Game Balance Optimization

One notable application of machine learning in games is balancing. Game balance is crucial to providing a fair and enjoyable experience for players. ML algorithms can analyze player data to identify overpowered or underpowered characters, weapons, or abilities. Game developers can then use this feedback to make data-driven adjustments, leading to a more balanced gameplay experience.

Future Prospects

As machine learning continues to advance, its role in game AI is expected to grow. Developers will likely use ML to create more realistic, adaptive, and engaging game worlds, NPCs, and player experiences. Furthermore, as hardware capabilities improve, real-time machine learning in games will become more prevalent, enabling even more complex and dynamic AI-driven interactions.

In conclusion, machine learning is a powerful tool for enhancing game AI and player experiences. By leveraging ML techniques, game developers can create more immersive, challenging, and personalized gameplay, ultimately pushing the boundaries of interactive entertainment.

Chapter 16: Virtual and Augmented Reality

Section 16.1: VR and AR Basics in OpenGL

Virtual Reality (VR) and Augmented Reality (AR) have gained significant attention in recent years for their immersive and interactive experiences. This section provides an introduction to the basics of VR and AR development using OpenGL, a popular graphics library.

Understanding Virtual Reality (VR)

VR is a technology that immerses users in a computer-generated environment, typically using a head-mounted display (HMD) or VR headset. The goal is to create a sense of presence, where users feel like they are physically present in the virtual world. Key elements of VR development in OpenGL include:

1. Rendering for VR:

- VR rendering requires rendering two different views, one for each eye, to create a stereoscopic 3D effect. This is known as stereoscopic rendering.

- Distortion correction is applied to the rendered images to compensate for the lens distortion in VR headsets.

2. Head Tracking:

- VR headsets are equipped with sensors to track the user's head movements. This data is used to update the view in real-time to match the user's head position and orientation.

- In OpenGL, this involves adjusting the camera perspective based on the headset's sensor data.

3. Motion Controllers:

- Many VR systems come with motion controllers that allow users to interact with the virtual environment. These controllers are tracked in 3D space and can be used to simulate hands or other input devices.

- Implementing input handling for motion controllers is a crucial aspect of VR development.

Exploring Augmented Reality (AR)

AR overlays digital content onto the real world, typically viewed through a smartphone or AR glasses. Unlike VR, AR does not aim to replace the real world but enhances it. Key considerations for AR development with OpenGL include:

1. Camera Integration:

- AR relies on the device's camera to capture the real-world environment. This camera feed is used as the background onto which digital content is overlaid.

- OpenGL can be used to render 3D objects or annotations onto the camera feed, aligning them with the real world.

2. *Tracking and Recognition:*

- AR applications often require marker tracking or image recognition to identify objects or surfaces in the real world. Once recognized, digital content can be anchored to these markers.

- OpenGL can render digital content accurately in relation to the recognized markers.

OpenGL for VR and AR

OpenGL provides the graphics rendering capabilities needed for both VR and AR applications. Developers can use OpenGL to render 3D scenes, apply shaders for realistic effects, and handle the complexities of stereoscopic rendering. Additionally, OpenGL's cross-platform support makes it suitable for a wide range of VR and AR devices.

In conclusion, VR and AR development using OpenGL offers exciting possibilities for creating immersive and interactive experiences. Whether you're building a virtual world in VR or enhancing the real world with digital content in AR, OpenGL provides the foundation for delivering compelling visual experiences to users. This chapter will delve deeper into the technical aspects of VR and AR development, including rendering techniques, input handling, and performance optimization.

Section 16.2: Tracking and Input Systems

In the realm of Virtual Reality (VR) and Augmented Reality (AR) development, effective tracking and input systems are fundamental to providing users with immersive and interactive experiences. This section focuses on the critical aspects of tracking and input for VR and AR applications built using OpenGL.

Head Tracking in VR

Head tracking is a cornerstone of VR experiences. It enables users to look around within the virtual environment, providing a strong sense of presence. In OpenGL-based VR applications, head tracking is implemented through the following steps:

1. **Sensor Data:** VR headsets are equipped with various sensors, such as gyroscopes and accelerometers, to track head movements accurately. These sensors continuously provide data on the headset's orientation and position.
2. **Integration with OpenGL:** OpenGL is used to adjust the camera's perspective and position based on the sensor data. This synchronization ensures that the rendered scene aligns with the user's head movements in real-time.
3. **Low Latency:** Achieving low latency in head tracking is crucial to prevent motion sickness. VR developers work to minimize the delay between head movement and the updated view in the headset.
4. **Stereoscopic Rendering:** As mentioned in the previous section, VR applications render two separate views—one for each eye. Head tracking ensures that each eye receives the correct perspective, creating a 3D effect.

Motion Controllers in VR

Motion controllers play a vital role in VR applications by allowing users to interact with the virtual environment. Key points to consider when implementing motion controllers in OpenGL-based VR include:

1. **Controller Tracking:** VR systems employ external tracking methods, such as cameras or infrared sensors, to precisely track the position and orientation of motion controllers. This tracking data is then integrated into the OpenGL scene.
2. **Input Mapping:** Developers map controller inputs, such as button presses or gestures, to specific actions in the VR application. For example, a trigger squeeze might simulate grabbing an object in the virtual world.
3. **Haptic Feedback:** Many modern VR controllers provide haptic feedback, allowing users to feel vibrations or resistance corresponding to in-game events. Implementing haptic feedback enhances immersion.
4. **Interaction Physics:** The physics of virtual interactions must closely mimic real-world behavior. This involves handling collisions, object manipulation, and physics simulations based on controller input.

Augmented Reality Input

In AR applications, input methods differ from VR due to the mixed-reality nature of AR. Considerations for AR input systems include:

1. **Touchscreen Interactions:** AR experiences are often built for smartphones or AR glasses with touchscreens. Users interact by tapping, swiping, or gesturing on the screen.
2. **Gesture Recognition:** Advanced AR systems can recognize hand gestures or finger movements, allowing users to interact with digital objects or control the AR application with gestures.
3. **Voice and Speech Recognition:** Voice commands are another input method in AR. Speech recognition

technology can enable users to control the AR app or retrieve information through voice commands.

4. **Markerless Tracking:** AR applications sometimes use markerless tracking techniques to detect and track real-world objects without relying on predefined markers.

OpenGL's role in AR input is primarily related to rendering digital content and ensuring its alignment with the real world. The integration of sensor data, whether from smartphone sensors or external devices, is crucial for accurate AR tracking.

In summary, tracking and input systems are at the heart of VR and AR development. Whether it's providing seamless head tracking in VR or creating intuitive interaction methods in AR, developers must carefully design and implement these systems to deliver compelling and immersive experiences to users.

Section 16.3: Rendering for VR Headsets

Rendering for Virtual Reality (VR) headsets is a complex and specialized task that requires careful consideration of performance, stereoscopy, and user comfort. In this section, we will explore the key aspects of rendering content for VR experiences using OpenGL.

Stereoscopic Rendering

One of the fundamental principles of VR rendering is stereoscopy, which simulates depth perception by providing a slightly different view for each eye. In OpenGL, this involves rendering the scene twice, once for the left eye and once for the right eye. Here's how it's typically done:

1. **Two Cameras:** To create the stereoscopic effect, you need two cameras—one for each eye. These cameras have

slightly different positions and orientations to simulate the separation between human eyes.

2. **Render Passes:** During rendering, your OpenGL application performs two separate render passes. In each pass, the scene is drawn from the perspective of one of the cameras. The resulting images are then sent to the respective eye in the VR headset.

3. **Synchronization:** It's crucial to ensure synchronization between the two render passes to avoid visual discomfort. This includes synchronizing camera movements and any dynamic elements in the scene.

Field of View (FOV) and Performance

VR headsets have a limited field of view (FOV), which means that only a portion of the scene needs to be rendered at high detail. Rendering everything in high detail can be computationally expensive and may lead to performance issues. To optimize VR rendering:

1. **FOV Culling:** Implement culling techniques to determine which parts of the scene are visible within the headset's FOV. Only render what the user can see to improve performance.

2. **Dynamic Resolution:** Some VR systems support dynamic resolution scaling. When the application detects a drop in frame rate, it can automatically reduce the resolution to maintain a smooth experience.

3. **Asynchronous Timewarp (ATW):** ATW is a technique used by VR systems to reduce latency. It reprojects frames in real-time to match the headset's current orientation, compensating for any rendering delays.

Distortion Correction

VR headsets use lenses to magnify the display, which can introduce distortion. To counteract this distortion and provide a correct view to the user, you'll need to apply distortion correction. OpenGL shaders can help with this process. Distortion correction shaders modify the rendered image to counteract the lens-induced distortion, ensuring that straight lines appear straight in the headset.

Performance Considerations

Performance is a critical factor in VR rendering. Achieving a consistent frame rate, typically 90 frames per second (FPS) or higher, is crucial to prevent motion sickness and provide a comfortable experience. Here are some performance considerations:

1. **GPU Performance:** VR rendering places a heavy load on the GPU. Optimizing shaders, reducing overdraw, and minimizing texture memory usage are essential.
2. **CPU Performance:** The CPU must handle tracking data, physics simulations, and other tasks. Multithreading can help distribute the workload efficiently.
3. **Memory Usage:** VR applications should be mindful of memory usage to avoid stuttering or crashes. Proper memory management is essential.
4. **Latency Reduction:** Minimizing input-to-display latency is vital for user comfort. This involves optimizing every step of the rendering pipeline, from input processing to display synchronization.

In conclusion, rendering for VR headsets in OpenGL involves specialized techniques to create a stereoscopic, distortion-free, and high-performance experience. Developers must carefully manage resources, optimize rendering, and ensure low-latency interactions to provide immersive VR experiences that users can enjoy comfortably for extended periods.

Section 16.4: AR Scene Recognition and Placement

Augmented Reality (AR) is a technology that overlays digital content onto the real world, creating interactive and immersive experiences. One of the key challenges in AR development is recognizing and placing virtual objects in the physical environment. In this section, we will explore the techniques and considerations for AR scene recognition and object placement.

AR Scene Recognition

Scene recognition in AR involves identifying the physical environment and understanding its characteristics. This is essential for anchoring virtual content accurately within the real world. Here are some common techniques and technologies used for AR scene recognition:

1. **SLAM (Simultaneous Localization and Mapping):** SLAM is a fundamental technology in AR. It allows devices to simultaneously create a map of the physical environment and determine their position within that environment. SLAM can use visual, depth, or sensor data to achieve this.
2. **Computer Vision:** Computer vision algorithms can analyze camera images or video streams to identify landmarks, objects, or patterns in the environment. These visual cues can be used for precise object placement.
3. **Depth Sensing:** Depth sensors, such as LiDAR (Light Detection and Ranging), provide accurate depth

information about the surroundings. This data is valuable for understanding the 3D structure of the environment.

Object Placement

Once the AR system recognizes the physical environment, the next step is to place virtual objects within it convincingly. This involves determining the position, orientation, and scale of virtual objects relative to the real world. Here are key considerations for object placement in AR:

1. **Tracking and Calibration:** Accurate tracking of the AR device is critical. Devices may use GPS, accelerometers, gyroscopes, or external tracking systems like fiducial markers to maintain precise position and orientation information.

2. **Anchoring:** Virtual objects need to be anchored to specific points or planes in the real world. Common anchor points include surfaces (tables, floors), objects (posters, signs), or even the user's hand.

3. **Interaction:** Consider how users will interact with virtual objects. Gesture recognition, touch input, or voice commands can be integrated into AR applications for user interaction.

4. **Realistic Lighting and Shadows:** To enhance the realism of virtual objects, they should cast and receive shadows that match the lighting conditions of the physical environment.

AR Frameworks and Tools

Developing AR applications from scratch can be complex. Fortunately, there are AR frameworks and tools available that streamline the development process. Some popular AR platforms and SDKs include:

- **ARKit (iOS)**: Apple's ARKit is a framework for building AR apps on iOS devices. It provides scene understanding, object placement, and interaction tools.

- **ARCore (Android)**: Google's ARCore is the Android equivalent of ARKit, offering similar capabilities for Android devices.

- **Unity and Unreal Engine**: These popular game engines have AR extensions that allow developers to create AR experiences using familiar tools.

Challenges and Future Directions

AR scene recognition and object placement continue to evolve. Challenges such as occlusion (virtual objects hiding behind real-world objects) and seamless integration of AR into daily life remain areas of active research. The development of AR glasses and wearable devices is also expected to open up new possibilities for AR applications.

In conclusion, AR scene recognition and object placement are essential components of creating compelling AR experiences. Developers can leverage AR frameworks and tools to streamline the development process, but understanding the underlying technologies and considerations is crucial for building successful AR applications. As AR technology advances, it is likely to play an increasingly significant role in various industries, from gaming and education to healthcare and retail.

Section 16.5: Performance and Optimization

for VR/AR

Performance and optimization are critical aspects of developing Virtual Reality (VR) and Augmented Reality (AR) applications. These immersive technologies demand high frame rates and low latency to provide users with a comfortable and convincing experience. In this section, we will explore key considerations and optimization techniques for VR/AR development.

1. Frame Rate and Latency

Maintaining a high and consistent frame rate is paramount in VR/AR. A lower frame rate can lead to motion sickness and discomfort. For VR, a frame rate of 90 frames per second (FPS) or higher is typically recommended. AR applications also benefit from higher frame rates to ensure smooth interactions with the real world.

Latency, or the delay between user input and the corresponding visual or auditory feedback, should be minimized. High latency can lead to disorientation and nausea in VR. Techniques such as predictive tracking and asynchronous time warp can help reduce latency.

2. Level of Detail (LOD)

Implementing level of detail (LOD) techniques is crucial for optimizing 3D scenes. In VR/AR, where real-time rendering is essential, LOD helps manage the complexity of 3D models. Objects in the distance can be rendered with lower detail to save processing power while maintaining visual quality for nearby objects.

3. Occlusion Culling

Occlusion culling involves determining which objects are not visible to the camera and therefore do not need to be rendered. This technique is especially important in AR, where virtual objects need to interact with the real world seamlessly. Proper occlusion culling reduces rendering load and improves performance.

4. Texture Compression

Texture compression techniques reduce memory usage and improve rendering speed. This is important for mobile VR/AR devices, which often have limited hardware resources. Modern GPUs support various texture compression formats like ETC2, ASTC, and PVRTC.

5. Asynchronous Compute

Asynchronous compute is a feature available on some GPUs that allows certain tasks to run independently, improving overall performance. It can be used for tasks like physics simulations or post-processing effects while the main rendering thread continues its work.

6. Adaptive Quality

Adaptive quality techniques adjust rendering quality on the fly based on the device's performance capabilities. When the device struggles to maintain the target frame rate, adaptive quality can automatically reduce rendering quality to prioritize smooth performance.

7. GPU and CPU Optimization

Profiling and optimizing GPU and CPU usage is crucial. GPU optimization includes reducing overdraw, minimizing draw calls, and using GPU instancing. CPU optimization involves efficient scripting and minimizing unnecessary calculations.

8. Battery Life

For mobile VR/AR devices, optimizing battery life is essential. This includes efficient use of hardware resources, minimizing background processes, and implementing power-saving features.

9. Testing and Benchmarking

Thorough testing and benchmarking on target devices are essential to identify performance bottlenecks. Tools like Unity's Profiler and Android's GPU Profiler can help pinpoint issues.

10. Update Frequency

Consider the update frequency of tracking data and sensor inputs. Higher update frequencies can provide smoother interactions but may demand more processing power. Finding the right balance is crucial.

In conclusion, achieving optimal performance in VR/AR development requires a combination of hardware-aware optimization techniques and a deep understanding of the target devices. Developers should continuously test and iterate to ensure that their applications run smoothly on a variety of VR/AR platforms. As VR and AR technology advances, optimizing for performance will remain a central concern, enabling the creation of increasingly immersive and compelling experiences.

Chapter 17: Tools, Editors, and Middleware

This chapter delves into the various tools, editors, and middleware commonly used in game development. These essential components aid developers in creating, optimizing, and managing their games efficiently.

Section 17.1: Introduction to Game Engines

Game engines are foundational software frameworks that provide the essential building blocks for creating games. They simplify and streamline the game development process, offering a wide range of features and tools. Here, we'll explore the fundamental concepts of game engines.

What Is a Game Engine?

A game engine is a comprehensive software framework designed to facilitate game development. It includes a set of tools, libraries, and systems that handle core functionalities like rendering, physics, audio, scripting, and more. Game engines aim to simplify the development process, allowing developers to focus on game-specific features.

Key Components of a Game Engine

1. **Rendering Engine**: Responsible for rendering graphics and managing visual effects. It handles 2D and 3D graphics, shaders, lighting, and rendering pipelines.
2. **Physics Engine**: Simulates physical interactions within the game world, such as collisions, gravity, and object dynamics.
3. **Audio Engine**: Manages sound effects, music, and spatial audio for an immersive auditory experience.
4. **Scripting Engine**: Allows developers to write scripts or code to control game behavior. Often supports scripting languages like Lua, Python, or custom languages.
5. **Asset Management**: Handles the organization and loading of game assets, including textures, models, and audio files.
6. **Input Handling**: Manages user input from various devices

like keyboards, mice, gamepads, and touch screens.

7. **AI Framework**: Provides tools for implementing artificial intelligence, including pathfinding, decision-making, and behavior trees.

8. **Networking**: Enables multiplayer functionality and communication between players in online games.

9. **Editor and IDE**: Offers a user-friendly interface for designing and editing game levels, assets, and scripts. Integrated development environments (IDEs) often accompany game engines.

Popular Game Engines

There are several game engines available, each with its strengths and specialties:

- **Unity**: Known for its accessibility and versatility, Unity is widely used for 2D and 3D game development across various platforms.

- **Unreal Engine**: Renowned for its high-quality graphics and photorealistic rendering, Unreal Engine is a top choice for AAA titles and advanced simulations.

- **Godot Engine**: An open-source engine that's beginner-friendly and ideal for 2D and 3D game development.

- **CryEngine**: Famous for its stunning visuals, CryEngine is used in many first-person shooters and open-world games.

- **Lumberyard**: Developed by Amazon, Lumberyard offers deep integration with AWS (Amazon Web Services) and is suitable for creating online multiplayer games.

- **Custom Engines**: Some studios opt to build their proprietary engines tailored to their specific game requirements.

Engine Selection

When choosing a game engine, consider factors like project scope, target platforms, team expertise, and licensing costs. It's crucial to select an engine that aligns with your project's needs and goals.

In summary, game engines are instrumental in game development, providing essential tools and systems to create immersive gaming experiences. Each engine has its unique features and advantages, making the choice of engine a significant decision in the development process.

Section 17.2: Integrating with Physics Middleware

Physics middleware plays a critical role in game development, as it's responsible for simulating realistic physical interactions within the game world. While game engines often come with built-in physics engines, some projects may require more advanced or specialized physics simulations. In such cases, integrating third-party physics middleware becomes necessary.

The Role of Physics Middleware

Physics middleware is a software component that focuses exclusively on simulating physical phenomena, such as gravity, collisions, rigid body dynamics, and soft body deformations. It provides game developers with a set of tools and APIs to create realistic physics interactions, which greatly enhance the immersion and gameplay of a video game.

Benefits of Physics Middleware

1. **Realism**: Physics middleware allows developers to model real-world physical behavior, making in-game objects and characters move, collide, and interact convincingly.
2. **Efficiency**: Physics middleware often employs optimized algorithms and data structures, ensuring efficient real-time performance, even in complex scenes.
3. **Customization**: Middleware solutions are often highly configurable, enabling developers to fine-tune physics behavior to suit their specific game requirements.
4. **Cross-platform**: Many physics middleware libraries support multiple platforms and game engines, providing flexibility for game development across various devices.

Popular Physics Middleware Solutions

Several physics middleware options are available for game developers. Here are a few notable ones:

NVIDIA PhysX

NVIDIA PhysX is a widely used physics middleware known for its performance and stability. It offers features like rigid body dynamics, character controllers, cloth simulation, and particle systems. It's been used in numerous AAA titles and supports integration with popular game engines like Unity and Unreal Engine.

Havok Physics

Havok Physics is a robust middleware solution with a strong track record in the gaming industry. It provides advanced physics simulations for characters, objects, and vehicles, along with tools for debugging and profiling. Havok Physics has been used in many high-profile games.

Bullet Physics

Bullet Physics is an open-source physics middleware library that's popular for its flexibility and affordability. It includes features like rigid body and soft body dynamics, collision detection, and constraints. Bullet Physics has been used in both indie and AAA games and supports various game engines.

NVIDIA FleX

NVIDIA FleX is a middleware library specializing in soft body and particle-based simulations. It's particularly well-suited for simulating deformable objects, fluids, and cloth. FleX is known for its scalability and ability to handle large-scale simulations.

Integrating Physics Middleware

Integrating physics middleware into a game engine involves several steps:

1. **Library Integration**: Begin by adding the physics

middleware library to your project. This typically includes linking the library and including the necessary header files.

2. **Initialization**: Initialize the physics middleware in your game code, setting up parameters such as gravity, time step, and collision settings.

3. **Creating Objects**: Define the physical properties of in-game objects, such as mass, shape, and collision properties. Attach these properties to the corresponding game objects.

4. **Simulation**: Update the physics simulation each frame, allowing the middleware to calculate new positions and orientations for objects based on physical interactions.

5. **Collision Handling**: Detect and respond to collisions between objects, implementing appropriate behaviors such as bouncing, sliding, or deformation.

6. **Integration with Game Logic**: Integrate the physics simulation with your game's logic, ensuring that physics interactions affect gameplay and player experiences.

7. **Debugging and Testing**: Thoroughly test the physics interactions in your game, using debugging tools provided by the middleware to identify and resolve issues.

8. **Performance Optimization**: Optimize the performance of the physics simulation to ensure smooth gameplay, considering techniques like spatial partitioning and multi-threading.

9. **Documentation**: Document the integration process and physics settings for future reference and collaboration within the development team.

When integrating physics middleware, it's essential to refer to the middleware's documentation and seek support from the middleware's community or support channels as needed. This ensures a successful integration that enhances the realism and quality of your game's physics interactions.

Section 17.3: Building Custom Tools and Editors

Game development involves not only creating the game itself but also building a suite of tools and editors to streamline the development process. These custom tools are essential for tasks such as level design, asset management, debugging, and performance profiling. In this section, we'll explore the importance of custom tools and the process of creating them.

The Role of Custom Tools

Custom tools and editors serve several crucial functions in game development:

1. **Efficiency**: Custom tools automate repetitive tasks, reducing the time and effort required to create, edit, and manage game assets and content.
2. **Workflow Optimization**: They streamline the development workflow, making it easier for artists, designers, and programmers to collaborate and iterate on game elements.
3. **Debugging and Testing**: Custom debugging tools provide insights into the game's behavior, helping developers identify and fix issues more efficiently.
4. **Content Creation**: Level editors, terrain generators, and asset importers simplify the creation of in-game content, such as levels, characters, and animations.
5. **Performance Profiling**: Profiling tools allow developers to analyze the game's performance and optimize it for target

platforms.

6. **User Interface Design**: Custom editors enable the design and arrangement of user interfaces, making it possible to create in-game menus and HUDs.

Types of Custom Tools

1. **Level Editors**: Level editors are crucial for creating game worlds. They allow designers to place objects, terrain, and assets, and define gameplay elements like triggers and waypoints.

2. **Asset Management Tools**: Asset management tools organize and categorize game assets, making it easy to locate and modify textures, models, sounds, and scripts.

3. **Animation Tools**: These tools assist in creating and editing character animations, including rigging, keyframing, and blending animations.

4. **Shader Editors**: For graphics programmers, shader editors provide a visual interface to create and fine-tune shaders, enhancing the game's visual quality.

5. **Debugging Tools**: Debugging tools help locate and diagnose issues in the game code, allowing for quicker problem resolution.

6. **Performance Profilers**: Profiling tools analyze the game's performance, identifying bottlenecks and resource-intensive operations that need optimization.

Building Custom Tools

Creating custom tools typically involves the following steps:

1. **Identify Needs**: Determine which aspects of the development process could benefit from custom tools.

Collaborate with the development team to gather requirements.

2. **Choose a Platform**: Decide whether the tools will be standalone applications, integrated into the game engine, or web-based. Select a programming language and framework accordingly.

3. **Design the User Interface**: Plan the tool's user interface (UI) to be intuitive and user-friendly. Consider the needs of artists, designers, and programmers who will use the tool.

4. **Develop Functionality**: Write the code to implement the tool's features and functionality. Depending on the tool's complexity, this may involve creating UI elements, handling file I/O, and processing data.

5. **Testing and Debugging**: Thoroughly test the tool to ensure it functions correctly. Debug any issues and refine the tool's performance and usability.

6. **Documentation**: Document the tool's usage, features, and any customization options. This documentation aids users and future developers who maintain or extend the tool.

7. **User Feedback**: Collect feedback from the development team and iterate on the tool based on their input.

8. **Integration**: If necessary, integrate the custom tools into the game engine's development environment or workflow.

9. **Version Control**: Place the tools under version control to track changes and collaborate with team members effectively.

Custom tools and editors are invaluable assets in game development, contributing to faster development cycles, improved collaboration, and higher-quality games. Building these tools requires careful planning, development, and ongoing maintenance to ensure they meet the evolving needs of the development team.

Section 17.4: Scripting and Automation

Scripting and automation play a crucial role in game development, allowing developers to streamline repetitive tasks, extend the functionality of tools and editors, and implement gameplay features quickly. In this section, we'll explore how scripting languages and automation can enhance the game development process.

The Role of Scripting

Scripting languages, such as Python, Lua, and JavaScript, are commonly used in game development for various purposes:

1. **Workflow Automation**: Scripts automate repetitive tasks, such as asset import, data processing, and build pipeline management. This reduces manual work and minimizes errors.
2. **Custom Tools**: Scripting enables the creation of custom tools and editors that extend the functionality of the game engine or development environment.
3. **Gameplay Logic**: Many game engines support scripting for implementing gameplay logic, allowing designers to define behaviors, events, and interactions without modifying the core engine code.
4. **Modding Support**: Scripting languages facilitate modding by providing an accessible way for players and modders to modify and extend a game's functionality.
5. **Prototyping**: Rapid prototyping of game mechanics and features is possible through scripting, enabling quick experimentation and iteration.

Benefits of Scripting

1. Flexibility: Scripting languages are flexible and dynamic, allowing developers to make changes on-the-fly without recompiling the entire game.

2. Accessibility: Non-programmers, such as designers and artists, can use scripting to create and modify content, making development more inclusive.

3. Debugging: Scripts are usually easier to debug than compiled code because issues can be identified and fixed without a full rebuild.

4. Iteration Speed: Script changes take effect immediately, speeding up the iteration process during development.

5. Community and Mods: Game communities often embrace scripting, leading to the creation of mods, extensions, and user-generated content that can extend a game's lifespan.

Scripting in Game Engines

Many game engines provide built-in support for scripting, often using languages like Lua or Python. For example:

- **Unity**: Supports C# for gameplay scripting, but also allows integration of external scripting languages like Python through plugins.

- **Unreal Engine**: Utilizes a visual scripting system called Blueprints in addition to C++ scripting.

- **Godot**: Offers its own scripting language, GDScript, which is similar to Python, along with support for C# and VisualScript.

Automation with Build Systems

In addition to scripting, build systems and automation tools are essential for managing the game's build and deployment process. Tools like Jenkins, Travis CI, and custom build scripts automate tasks such as:

- **Compilation**: Automatically compile source code into executable binaries for different platforms.

- **Asset Pipeline**: Optimize and package game assets for distribution.

- **Testing**: Execute unit tests, integration tests, and performance tests automatically.

- **Deployment**: Deploy game builds to various platforms, such as PC, consoles, and mobile devices.

Example of Workflow Automation

Here's a simple example of using Python to automate a common game development task: asset conversion.

```python
import os

from PIL import Image
# Define the input and output directories
input_dir = "raw_textures"
```

```python
output_dir = "processed_textures"

# Ensure the output directory exists

os.makedirs(output_dir, exist_ok=True)

# Iterate through input files

for filename in os.listdir(input_dir):

if filename.endswith(".png"):

# Load the image

image = Image.open(os.path.join(input_dir, filename))

# Apply a simple image processing operation

processed_image = image.convert("RGBA")

# Save the processed image to the output directory

processed_image.save(os.path.join(output_dir, filename))

print("Asset conversion complete.")
```

This Python script takes images from the raw_textures directory, processes them (in this case, converting them to RGBA format), and saves the processed images in the processed_textures directory. This automation simplifies the asset preparation workflow.

In conclusion, scripting and automation are indispensable tools in modern game development. They empower developers, streamline workflows, and enable rapid iteration and content creation. Whether for gameplay scripting, tool creation, or build automation, scripting languages and automation tools significantly contribute to the efficiency and success of game development projects.

Section 17.5: Asset Pipelines and Workflows

Efficient asset management is a critical aspect of game development. Assets include everything from 3D models, textures, and audio files to scripts, animations, and level data. In this section, we will explore asset pipelines and workflows, which are essential for organizing, creating, importing, and managing game assets effectively.

The Role of Asset Pipelines

An asset pipeline is a set of processes and tools used to handle game assets from their creation to their integration into the game. The key objectives of an asset pipeline are as follows:

1. **Consistency**: Ensure that all assets adhere to a consistent format and quality standard.
2. **Optimization**: Optimize assets for performance without compromising quality.
3. **Version Control**: Maintain a version history of assets, enabling collaboration and tracking changes.
4. **Integration**: Seamlessly integrate assets into the game engine or editor.
5. **Automation**: Automate repetitive tasks such as asset conversion, compression, and packaging.

Asset Workflow Stages

Asset pipelines typically consist of several stages, each serving a specific purpose:

1. **Asset Creation**: Artists, designers, and sound engineers create assets using specialized software like 3D modeling tools, image editors, or audio workstations.
2. **Export**: Assets are exported from their creation software

into a format suitable for game development. This may involve converting models to a game-ready format or exporting textures in the correct size and compression.

3. **Import**: Assets are imported into the game engine or development environment. Metadata, such as textures' import settings or animation clips, is configured during this stage.

4. **Processing**: Some assets require additional processing, such as texture compression, LOD generation, or audio format conversion. This stage aims to optimize assets for runtime performance.

5. **Integration**: Assets are integrated into the game's scenes, levels, or scripts. This involves linking models to entities, assigning textures to materials, or attaching scripts to game objects.

6. **Version Control**: Asset files are managed using version control systems (e.g., Git) to track changes, collaborate with team members, and ensure consistency.

7. **Build Pipeline**: As part of the build process, assets are packaged and prepared for distribution. This might include packing textures into texture atlases, generating asset bundles, or creating build-specific asset configurations.

Best Practices for Asset Pipelines

To ensure a smooth asset workflow, consider the following best practices:

1. Asset Naming Conventions: Establish clear naming conventions for assets to make them easily identifiable and maintainable.

2. Folder Structure: Organize assets into a structured directory hierarchy. Use folders for textures, models, audio, scripts, and other asset types.

3. Metadata and Documentation: Include metadata files or documentation that describe asset-specific details, such as usage instructions or dependencies.

4. Backup and Versioning: Regularly back up assets and use version control systems to track changes and revert to previous states if needed.

5. Collaboration: Implement collaboration tools that allow team members to work on assets concurrently without conflicts.

6. Asset Validation: Use automated validation scripts or tools to check asset integrity, detect errors, and ensure assets meet performance requirements.

7. Asset Compression: Utilize compression and optimization techniques to reduce asset file sizes while maintaining quality.

Example Asset Pipeline Script

Here's a simplified Python script that demonstrates how an asset pipeline tool might automate the process of compressing textures using a tool like pngquant:

```python
import os

import subprocess

# Define input and output directories
input_dir = "raw_textures"
```

```python
output_dir = "compressed_textures"

# Ensure the output directory exists

os.makedirs(output_dir, exist_ok=True)

# Iterate through input files

for filename in os.listdir(input_dir):

if filename.endswith(".png"):

# Compress the image using pngquant

input_path = os.path.join(input_dir, filename)

output_path = os.path.join(output_dir, filename)

subprocess.run(["pngquant", "—force", "—output", output_path,
input_path])

print("Texture compression complete.")
```

This script takes raw textures from the raw_textures directory, compresses them using pngquant, and saves the compressed versions in the compressed_textures directory, automating the texture compression process.

In conclusion, asset pipelines and workflows are indispensable components of game development. They ensure that assets are created, managed, and integrated efficiently, ultimately contributing to the success of a game project. By following best practices and automating asset-related tasks, development teams can streamline their workflows and maintain a high level of consistency and quality in their games.

Chapter 18: Optimization and Debugging

Section 18.1: Profiling Tools and Techniques

Profiling is a crucial aspect of game development that involves analyzing the performance of your game or application to identify bottlenecks and areas for optimization. Profiling tools help developers gain insights into various aspects of their code, such as CPU usage, memory usage, and frame rendering times. In this section, we'll explore profiling tools and techniques used to improve the performance of your games.

The Importance of Profiling

Profiling serves several essential purposes in game development:

1. **Performance Optimization**: Profiling helps you identify areas of your code that consume excessive CPU or memory resources. By pinpointing performance bottlenecks, you can optimize critical sections of your game to run more efficiently.

2. **Resource Management**: Profiling tools can reveal memory leaks, allowing you to address them promptly. Efficient memory management is vital for long-term stability and performance.

3. **Frame Rate Analysis**: Monitoring frame rendering times is crucial for ensuring a smooth and responsive gaming experience. Profiling helps you achieve consistent frame rates and avoid frame drops.

4. **Content Optimization**: Profiling can help you identify unused or redundant assets, allowing you to optimize

content loading and reduce storage requirements.

Profiling Tools

There are various profiling tools available for game developers, each focusing on different aspects of performance analysis. Some commonly used profiling tools include:

1. CPU Profilers: CPU profilers monitor the execution of your code, identifying functions or methods that consume the most processing time. Tools like Intel VTune, AMD CodeXL, and Xcode Instruments are popular CPU profiling options.

2. Memory Profilers: Memory profilers track memory allocations and deallocations, helping you detect memory leaks and excessive memory usage. Tools like Valgrind, Visual Studio's Memory Profiler, and Clang's AddressSanitizer are valuable for memory profiling.

3. GPU Profilers: GPU profilers analyze the performance of your graphics pipeline, including shader execution and GPU memory usage. NVIDIA's Nsight Graphics and AMD's Radeon GPU Profiler are examples of GPU profiling tools.

4. Frame Profilers: Frame profilers provide detailed information about each frame rendered by your game. They help identify rendering bottlenecks and frame time spikes. Unity's Frame Debugger and Unreal Engine's GPU Visualizer are examples of frame profiling tools.

5. Network Profilers: For multiplayer games, network profilers help analyze network traffic, latency, and packet loss. Wireshark and specialized game networking libraries often include network profiling features.

Profiling Techniques

Profiling involves more than just running a tool; it requires a systematic approach to uncover performance issues:

1. Instrumentation: Add profiling code to your application to measure specific functions or sections of code. This can be done manually or by using profiling libraries or macros.

2. Sampling: Profiling tools often use sampling to collect data periodically. Sampling involves taking snapshots of the program's state at predefined intervals, allowing you to analyze code execution and resource usage.

3. Analysis: After collecting profiling data, it's essential to analyze the results carefully. Look for patterns, hotspots, and outliers that indicate performance issues.

4. Optimization: Once you've identified bottlenecks or areas for improvement, apply optimization techniques to your code. This might involve algorithm changes, code refactoring, or adjusting rendering settings.

5. Iteration: Profiling is an iterative process. After making optimizations, re-run the profiling tools to verify improvements and identify new issues.

Profiling in Action

Here's a brief example of using Unity's Profiler, a frame profiler, to analyze frame rendering times in a Unity game:

```
void Update()

{

// Code for game logic

// Profiling section for measuring frame rendering times

Profiler.BeginSample("Render Frame");

// Code for rendering the frame

Profiler.EndSample();

}
```

In this example, we use Unity's Profiler API to profile the rendering of each frame. By wrapping the rendering code in a profiling sample, we can visualize the time taken by this part of the code in Unity's Profiler window.

In summary, profiling is an essential practice for optimizing game performance. By using the right profiling tools and techniques, developers can identify and address performance bottlenecks, resulting in smoother gameplay and improved user experiences. Profiling should be an integral part of your game development workflow, from initial development to post-release updates.

Section 18.2: Memory Management and Leaks

Memory management is a critical aspect of game development, and addressing memory leaks is vital for maintaining the stability and performance of your games. In this section, we'll delve into memory management techniques and how to identify and resolve memory leaks in your game code.

The Importance of Memory Management

Efficient memory management ensures that your game allocates and deallocates memory resources appropriately throughout its runtime. Failure to manage memory effectively can lead to several issues:

1. **Memory Leaks**: Memory leaks occur when your game allocates memory but doesn't release it when it's no longer needed. Over time, this can lead to increased memory usage and eventual crashes.
2. **Performance Degradation**: Inefficient memory usage can result in reduced performance, as the game's memory allocator struggles to find and allocate memory blocks.
3. **Stability Issues**: Excessive memory usage can destabilize your game, leading to crashes, freezes, or unresponsive behavior.

Memory Management Techniques

To maintain efficient memory usage and avoid memory leaks, consider the following techniques:

1. Use Smart Pointers: In languages like C++ and C#, smart pointers (e.g., std::shared_ptr, std::unique_ptr, std::weak_ptr in C++) help manage memory automatically. They automatically release memory when it's no longer referenced.

2. Manual Memory Management: In languages like C and C++, you can manually allocate and deallocate memory using functions like malloc() and free(). However, this approach requires careful tracking of memory allocations and deallocations.

3. Resource Management Systems: Implement resource

management systems to handle assets like textures, models, and sounds. These systems can load and unload resources as needed, reducing memory overhead.

4. Object Pooling: Use object pooling to recycle and reuse objects instead of constantly creating and destroying them. This reduces memory allocation and deallocation overhead.

5. Profile Memory Usage: Utilize memory profiling tools to monitor your game's memory usage during development. This helps identify potential leaks and excessive memory consumption.

Identifying Memory Leaks

Identifying memory leaks can be challenging, but memory profiling tools can assist in this process. Here's a general approach to identifying memory leaks:

1. Use Memory Profilers: Employ memory profiling tools specific to your development environment. Tools like Valgrind, Instruments (for macOS/iOS), or the Memory Profiler in Visual Studio can help.

2. Take Snapshots: While running your game in a profiling environment, take memory snapshots at different points during gameplay. This captures the memory state at specific times.

3. Analyze Allocations: Compare memory snapshots to identify memory allocations that consistently grow over time. Look for objects that are created but never released.

4. Check Reference Counts: In languages with garbage collection or reference counting, ensure that reference counts are decreasing when objects should be removed.

5. Review Code: Examine the code associated with identified memory leaks. Look for missing deallocations or circular references that prevent objects from being released.

6. Test Edge Cases: Test your game with extreme conditions or long play sessions to uncover memory leaks that may not be immediately apparent.

Resolving Memory Leaks

Once you've identified memory leaks, take steps to resolve them:

1. Fix Code Issues: Correct code that's causing memory leaks. Ensure that objects are properly deallocated when they're no longer needed.

2. Use RAII: In languages like C++, use Resource Acquisition Is Initialization (RAII) principles to manage resources automatically. Smart pointers and containers like std::vector can help.

3. Test Thoroughly: After making changes, retest your game to ensure that memory leaks have been addressed. Profiling tools can help confirm that leaks have been resolved.

4. Monitor Memory Usage: Continue to use memory profiling tools throughout development to catch new memory leaks as you add or modify code.

Effective memory management is an ongoing process in game development. By adopting best practices, using profiling tools, and diligently addressing memory leaks, you can maintain a stable and performant game that provides a seamless experience for players.

Section 18.3: Shader and Compute Optimization

Optimizing shaders and compute kernels is crucial for achieving optimal performance in graphics and compute applications. Shaders and compute kernels are responsible for a significant portion of the workload in modern graphics pipelines and general-purpose GPU computing. In this section, we'll explore various techniques and tips for optimizing shaders and compute kernels to ensure your applications run smoothly on GPUs.

1. Use Efficient Data Structures

One of the primary concerns when optimizing shaders and compute kernels is data access. Utilize efficient data structures like arrays, vectors, and matrices to store and access data. These structures are optimized for GPU processing and reduce memory access overhead.

2. Minimize Branching

Branching in shaders can be costly, as it can lead to divergent execution paths, where different threads take different code paths. Minimize conditional statements in your shaders and consider using conditional move instructions when possible to reduce branching overhead.

3. Utilize Loop Unrolling

Loop unrolling is a technique that can improve shader performance by manually expanding loops. This reduces loop overhead and allows the GPU to execute more instructions in parallel. However, be cautious not to unroll loops excessively, as it can lead to increased register pressure.

4. Optimize Memory Access

Efficient memory access patterns are essential for shader and compute kernel optimization. Use coalesced memory access, where threads access contiguous memory locations, to maximize memory throughput. Minimize global memory access and prefer shared or local memory when appropriate.

5. Consider Precision

Adjust the precision of your calculations based on your application's requirements. Reducing precision (e.g., using lowp instead of mediump or highp in GLSL) can significantly improve shader performance, but it may affect visual quality in some cases.

6. Batch Processing

Whenever possible, batch similar operations together to reduce redundant work. For example, when applying the same shader to multiple objects with the same material properties, group them together and render them in a single draw call.

7. Cull Unnecessary Work

Implement frustum culling and occlusion culling techniques to skip rendering objects or parts of the scene that are not visible. This reduces the workload on shaders and compute kernels.

8. Use Compute Shaders

Consider using compute shaders for non-graphics tasks that can benefit from GPU parallelism. Compute shaders allow you to harness the power of the GPU for a wide range of data processing tasks beyond traditional graphics.

9. Profile and Benchmark

Profiling and benchmarking are essential steps in shader and compute optimization. Use GPU profiling tools to identify performance bottlenecks and hotspots in your shaders and compute kernels.

10. Experiment and Iterate

Optimization is an iterative process. Experiment with different optimizations, measure their impact on performance, and iterate on your shader or kernel code to find the best balance between performance and visual quality.

11. Compiler Optimizations

Shader compilers are continually improving, and they can perform various optimizations automatically. Keep your graphics drivers and shader compilers up to date to take advantage of these optimizations.

12. Reduce Redundant Computations

Avoid redundant calculations in shaders. If a value is computed multiple times and doesn't change within a shader invocation, store it in a temporary variable to avoid recalculating it.

13. Leverage GPU Features

Modern GPUs offer various features like texture sampling, atomic operations, and thread synchronization. Understand these features and leverage them when appropriate to optimize your shaders and compute kernels.

14. Documentation and Profiling Tools

Refer to GPU documentation to understand the architecture-specific details and limitations of the GPU you're targeting. Additionally, use GPU profiling tools to gain insights into shader performance and bottlenecks.

Optimizing shaders and compute kernels can significantly impact the performance of your graphics and compute applications. By following these optimization techniques and continuously monitoring and profiling your code, you can ensure that your shaders and kernels run efficiently on a wide range of GPUs, providing a smooth and responsive user experience.

Section 18.4: Parallelism and Concurrency

Parallelism and concurrency are essential concepts in modern computer graphics and general-purpose GPU computing. They enable the efficient utilization of multi-core CPUs and massively parallel GPUs to perform tasks concurrently, leading to improved performance and responsiveness in graphics applications and compute workloads. In this section, we'll explore the concepts of parallelism and concurrency and how they can be leveraged for optimization.

1. Understanding Parallelism

Parallelism is the concept of breaking down a task into smaller subtasks that can be executed simultaneously by multiple processing units. In graphics programming, this often involves rendering multiple objects, processing pixels, or applying shaders concurrently.

2. Multi-threading for CPU Parallelism

Multi-threading is a common technique used to achieve CPU parallelism. In a multi-threaded application, different threads execute different parts of the program concurrently. For example, you can have one thread handling user input, another thread handling physics simulations, and a third thread responsible for rendering.

3. GPU Parallelism

Modern GPUs are highly parallel processors with thousands of cores. They excel at parallelizing tasks that can be broken down into independent subtasks. Graphics rendering, physics simulations, and compute-intensive operations can all benefit from GPU parallelism.

4. Thread Synchronization

When multiple threads or GPU cores access shared resources, proper synchronization is essential to avoid race conditions and data corruption. Techniques like mutexes, semaphores, and atomic operations ensure that threads or GPU cores coordinate their access to shared data.

5. Task Parallelism

Task parallelism involves dividing a program into independent tasks that can be executed in parallel. This approach is useful for parallelizing workloads that consist of many independent operations. Libraries like OpenMP and TBB (Threading Building Blocks) facilitate task parallelism in CPU-bound applications.

6. Data Parallelism

Data parallelism involves applying the same operation to multiple data elements concurrently. SIMD (Single Instruction, Multiple Data) instructions in CPUs and parallel processing in GPUs are well-suited for data parallelism. For example, when applying a shader to multiple vertices or pixels simultaneously, you're leveraging data parallelism.

7. Pipeline Parallelism

Pipeline parallelism divides a task into a series of stages, and each stage is executed in parallel. Graphics pipelines, which consist of vertex processing, geometry processing, fragment shading, and more, are classic examples of pipeline parallelism.

8. Asynchronous Execution

In graphics and compute applications, asynchronous execution allows tasks to be scheduled independently, maximizing resource utilization. For example, you can issue rendering commands, start GPU compute tasks, and read back results asynchronously, all while the CPU continues processing other tasks.

9. Optimizing for Parallelism

To harness the power of parallelism effectively, it's crucial to design your algorithms and data structures with parallelism in mind. Identify tasks that can be executed concurrently, minimize dependencies between tasks, and ensure efficient thread or GPU core synchronization.

10. Concurrency Challenges

While parallelism offers significant performance benefits, it also introduces challenges such as synchronization overhead, load balancing, and data coherence. These challenges must be carefully addressed to avoid performance bottlenecks.

11. GPU Compute Frameworks

For GPU-based parallelism and compute, frameworks like CUDA (for NVIDIA GPUs) and OpenCL (for various GPUs) provide tools and libraries for developing highly parallel GPU programs. These frameworks enable fine-grained control over GPU resources and parallel execution.

12. Hybrid Approaches

In some scenarios, a combination of CPU and GPU parallelism may be the most efficient solution. Hybrid approaches leverage the strengths of both CPU and GPU processing to achieve optimal performance.

Parallelism and concurrency are fundamental to achieving high performance in modern graphics and compute applications. By understanding these concepts and effectively designing your algorithms and code to exploit parallelism, you can unlock the full potential of multi-core CPUs and massively parallel GPUs, resulting in faster and more responsive applications.

Section 18.5: Advanced Debugging Techniques

Debugging is an integral part of software development, and in the context of computer graphics, it becomes even more critical due to the complexity of graphics applications. In this section, we'll explore advanced debugging techniques tailored to graphics programming and GPU-related issues.

1. GPU Debugging Tools

Modern graphics APIs, such as OpenGL and DirectX, provide debugging and profiling tools. These tools allow you to inspect the state of the GPU, set breakpoints in shaders, and visualize GPU performance metrics. For example, NVIDIA Nsight and AMD GPU PerfStudio are popular GPU debugging tools.

2. Shader Debugging

Debugging shaders can be challenging since they run on the GPU. However, some tools enable shader debugging by emulating shader execution on the CPU and providing interactive debugging capabilities. These tools help identify and fix shader-related issues effectively.

3. Frame Debugging

Frame debugging involves capturing and analyzing the state of your application frame by frame. You can inspect the state of resources, shaders, and draw calls at each frame, making it easier to identify rendering issues and performance bottlenecks.

4. Real-time Profiling

Profiling tools like NVIDIA Nsight, AMD Radeon GPU Profiler, and Intel GPA allow you to monitor GPU performance in real-time. You can identify GPU bottlenecks, measure frame times, and optimize your rendering pipeline accordingly.

5. API Validation Layers

Graphics APIs often include validation layers that check for errors and inconsistencies in your code. Enabling these layers during development can help catch issues early. For example, Vulkan offers validation layers that provide detailed error messages and warnings.

6. Capture and Replay

Some debugging tools offer capture and replay functionality, allowing you to record the entire frame's execution and replay it later for analysis. This feature is invaluable for tracking down hard-to-reproduce bugs.

7. Remote Debugging

Remote debugging enables you to debug graphics applications running on a remote machine or a target device. This is particularly useful for debugging graphics applications on consoles or mobile devices.

8. Instrumentation and Tracing

Instrumentation involves adding markers and trace events to your code. Tools like NVIDIA Nsight Graphics and RenderDoc can capture these events, providing a timeline view of your application's execution. This helps pinpoint performance bottlenecks.

9. Memory Debugging

Graphics applications often deal with complex memory management. Memory debugging tools can help detect memory leaks, buffer overflows, and other memory-related issues in your graphics code.

10. Crash Dumps and Minidumps

In the event of a crash, generating crash dumps or minidumps can capture the state of your application at the time of the crash. These dumps can be analyzed offline to determine the cause of the crash.

11. Code Analysis Tools

Static and dynamic code analysis tools can identify potential issues in your graphics code, such as uninitialized variables, dead code, and code paths that may lead to undefined behavior.

12. Community Resources

The graphics development community is rich with resources. Online forums, blogs, and community-driven projects often share solutions to common graphics programming problems. Leveraging these resources can help you troubleshoot issues effectively.

13. Continuous Integration (CI) and Testing

Implementing CI pipelines that build and test your graphics application regularly can catch issues early in the development process. Automated testing frameworks can also help ensure that changes do not introduce regressions.

14. Documentation and Comments

Thoroughly documenting your code and adding comments can make debugging easier, not just for you but also for your team members. Well-documented code helps everyone understand the intent and design of your graphics application.

Advanced debugging techniques are crucial for maintaining the stability and performance of graphics applications. By utilizing specialized tools, profiling, and debugging strategies tailored to graphics programming, you can effectively identify and resolve issues, ensuring your graphics application runs smoothly and efficiently.

Chapter 19: Cross-platform Considerations

Cross-platform development is essential in today's diverse gaming landscape, where games are played on various devices and operating systems. This chapter explores the challenges and strategies involved in making your graphics application or game work seamlessly across different platforms.

Section 19.1: Porting to Mobile and Consoles

Porting your graphics application or game to mobile devices and gaming consoles opens up new opportunities for reaching a broader audience. However, it comes with its unique set of challenges and considerations.

1. Platform-Specific APIs

Mobile devices and gaming consoles often have platform-specific graphics APIs. For example, Android uses OpenGL ES or Vulkan, while iOS uses Metal. Consoles like PlayStation and Xbox have their proprietary APIs. Porting involves rewriting or adapting your rendering code to work with these APIs.

2. Performance Optimization

Mobile devices and consoles have varying levels of hardware capabilities. To ensure smooth performance, you may need to optimize your code for each target platform. Techniques like dynamic quality scaling, LOD (Level of Detail), and reducing draw calls can help achieve good performance across different hardware.

3. Input Handling

Each platform has its unique input methods, such as touch controls for mobile and gamepad inputs for consoles. Your game should support and optimize for these input methods to provide an excellent user experience.

4. Screen Resolutions and Aspect Ratios

Mobile devices and consoles come in different screen sizes, resolutions, and aspect ratios. Your game's UI and rendering should adapt gracefully to these variations to avoid letterboxing or stretched graphics.

5. Memory Constraints

Mobile devices often have limited memory compared to PCs or consoles. Managing memory efficiently, optimizing texture sizes, and using texture compression are crucial to stay within the memory limits of target platforms.

6. Cross-Platform Libraries and Engines

Consider using cross-platform game engines and libraries like Unity, Unreal Engine, or Godot, which can simplify the porting process by handling many platform-specific details for you. These engines often offer support for various platforms out of the box.

7. Testing and QA

Thorough testing on each target platform is essential to catch platform-specific bugs and ensure a consistent gaming experience. This includes testing on various devices with different specifications and OS versions.

8. User Interface (UI) Adaptation

Adapting your game's UI to different screen sizes and input methods is crucial for providing an optimal user experience. Implement responsive UI layouts that can adjust to various screen resolutions and orientations.

9. Content Delivery

Consider how you'll deliver content updates and patches to users on different platforms. Each platform may have its content delivery system or restrictions on updates, so plan accordingly.

10. Legal and Licensing Considerations

Be aware of platform-specific legal and licensing requirements when publishing your game on consoles or mobile app stores. These requirements may include certification processes, content guidelines, and revenue-sharing agreements.

Porting your graphics application or game to mobile and console platforms can be challenging but rewarding. It allows you to tap into a broader audience and potentially increase your game's revenue. By carefully addressing the platform-specific considerations mentioned above and leveraging cross-platform tools and engines, you can successfully bring your game to a wide range of devices and operating systems.

Section 19.2: Dealing with Different OpenGL Versions

When developing graphics applications and games that target multiple platforms, you'll likely encounter differences in OpenGL (or OpenGL ES) versions and feature sets. Dealing with these variations is crucial for ensuring consistent performance and visual quality across platforms. In this section, we'll explore strategies for handling different OpenGL versions effectively.

1. Feature Detection

To work with different OpenGL versions, it's essential to detect the available features at runtime. OpenGL provides a way to query the supported extensions and capabilities of the current OpenGL context. You can use this information to enable or disable specific rendering techniques or features based on the capabilities of the user's hardware.

Here's an example of feature detection in OpenGL:

```
if (GLEW_VERSION_4_0) {

// Use OpenGL 4.0 features

glEnable(GL_SAMPLE_SHADING);

// ...

} else if (GLEW_VERSION_3_3) {

// Use OpenGL 3.3 features

glEnable(GL_MULTISAMPLE);

// ...

} else {

// Use fallback techniques for older OpenGL versions

// ...

}
```

2. Fallback Rendering Paths

When targeting older OpenGL versions, you may need to implement fallback rendering paths for features that aren't supported. For example, if a specific shader or rendering technique requires OpenGL 4.0 but your target platform only supports OpenGL 3.3, you can provide an alternative implementation that achieves a similar visual effect using the available features.

3. OpenGL Extensions

OpenGL extensions allow you to access additional features beyond the core OpenGL specification. You can use extensions to enable advanced capabilities on platforms that support them. However, it's crucial to handle extensions gracefully and provide fallbacks for platforms that don't support them.

4. Version-Independent Code

Write OpenGL code that is version-independent wherever possible. This means avoiding deprecated features and using modern OpenGL practices that are supported across a wide range of versions. Libraries like GLEW and GLFW can help manage OpenGL extensions and provide a consistent API across different platforms.

5. Shader Compatibility

Shaders play a significant role in graphics programming, and shader code can vary between OpenGL versions. When dealing with different OpenGL versions, ensure that your shaders are compatible and optimized for each target version. You may need to write separate shader programs or use preprocessor directives to conditionally compile shader code based on the OpenGL version.

6. Testing Across Platforms

Testing your graphics application or game on various platforms and OpenGL versions is crucial. It helps identify compatibility issues and ensures that your code behaves consistently. Consider setting up a testing pipeline that covers different GPUs, drivers, and operating systems.

7. Documentation and User Guidance

Clearly document the OpenGL requirements and supported versions for your graphics application or game. Provide guidance to users on how to update their graphics drivers or hardware if their system does not meet the minimum OpenGL version requirements.

8. Community Resources

Leverage community resources and forums where developers share their experiences with different OpenGL versions and platforms. These resources can provide valuable insights and solutions to common compatibility issues.

By adopting these strategies and being proactive in handling different OpenGL versions, you can develop graphics applications and games that are robust and compatible across a wide range of platforms, ensuring a smooth and consistent user experience regardless of the user's hardware or operating system.

Section 19.3: Platform-Specific Optimizations

When developing cross-platform games and graphics applications, it's essential to consider platform-specific optimizations. Different platforms have unique hardware architectures, APIs, and performance characteristics. By tailoring your code and assets to each platform, you can maximize performance and deliver a superior user experience. In this section, we'll explore various platform-specific optimizations you can apply to your projects.

1. Optimized Asset Loading

Each platform may have different file I/O performance characteristics. Optimize your asset loading code to take advantage of platform-specific file systems and storage devices. Consider using asynchronous loading techniques to keep your application responsive.

```
#ifdef _WIN32

// Windows-specific file loading code

// ...

#elif __APPLE__

// macOS and iOS-specific file loading code

// ...

#elif __linux__

// Linux-specific file loading code

// ...

#endif
```

2. Multithreading and Parallelism

Different platforms may have varying numbers of CPU cores and threading capabilities. Utilize multithreading and parallelism to distribute computational workloads efficiently. Platforms like Windows, macOS, and Linux offer different APIs for managing threads and synchronization. Be sure to use the appropriate threading model for each platform.

```
#ifdef _WIN32

// Windows-specific multithreading code

// ...

#elif __APPLE__

// macOS and iOS-specific multithreading code

// ...

#elif __linux__

// Linux-specific multithreading code

// ...

#endif
```

3. Graphics API Optimization

Each platform may use a different graphics API, such as DirectX on Windows, Metal on macOS/iOS, or Vulkan on Linux. Tailor your rendering code to leverage the strengths and features of the target graphics API. Implement platform-specific rendering optimizations when necessary.

```
#ifdef _WIN32

// Windows-specific rendering optimizations (DirectX)

// ...
```

```
#elif __APPLE__
```

// *macOS and iOS-specific rendering optimizations (Metal)*

// *...*

```
#elif __linux__
```

// *Linux-specific rendering optimizations (Vulkan)*

// *...*

```
#endif
```

4. Input Handling

Different platforms have varying input devices and event handling mechanisms. Implement platform-specific input handling code to provide seamless support for keyboards, mice, game controllers, touchscreens, and other input devices.

```
#ifdef _WIN32
```

// *Windows-specific input handling code*

// *...*

```
#elif __APPLE__
```

// *macOS and iOS-specific input handling code*

// *...*

```
#elif __linux__
```

// *Linux-specific input handling code*

// *...*

#endif

5. Audio Optimization

Optimize audio playback for the platform's audio subsystem. Windows, macOS, and Linux have different audio APIs and hardware support. Ensure that your audio code adapts to the platform's audio capabilities and performance characteristics.

#ifdef _WIN32

// Windows-specific audio optimization

// ...

#elif __APPLE__

// macOS and iOS-specific audio optimization

// ...

#elif __linux__

// Linux-specific audio optimization

// ...

#endif

6. Memory Management

Different platforms may have varying memory management constraints and behaviors. Implement platform-specific memory management kament techniques, taking into account memory allocation and deallocation patterns, as well as memory layout optimizations for cache efficiency.

#ifdef _WIN32

```
// Windows-specific memory management code

// ...

#elif __APPLE__

// macOS and iOS-specific memory management code

// ...

#elif __linux__

// Linux-specific memory management code

// ...

#endif
```

7. Performance Profiling

Use platform-specific profiling tools and performance analysis software to identify bottlenecks and optimize code. Platforms often provide specialized profiling tools that can help you pinpoint performance issues and make informed optimizations.

8. Platform-Specific Features

Leverage platform-specific features, such as platform-specific APIs, services, or hardware acceleration, to enhance your application's functionality and performance on each platform.

By following these platform-specific optimization strategies, you can ensure that your cross-platform games and graphics applications perform optimally on a variety of platforms, providing a consistent and satisfying experience for users on Windows, macOS, Linux, and other target platforms.

Section 19.4: Middleware and SDK Integration

Middleware and Software Development Kits (SDKs) play a crucial role in game development, offering pre-built solutions for various aspects of your game or graphics application. Integrating middleware and SDKs can significantly accelerate development, enhance functionality, and improve the overall quality of your project. In this section, we'll explore the importance of middleware and SDK integration and some common considerations when working with them.

1. What is Middleware?

Middleware refers to pre-built software components or libraries that provide specific functionality, such as physics simulation, audio processing, networking, and more. Game developers often integrate middleware to save time and resources while gaining access to professionally developed solutions.

2. Types of Middleware

There are various types of middleware available for game development:

- **Physics Middleware**: Middleware like NVIDIA PhysX and Havok offer realistic physics simulation for games, handling collision detection, rigid body dynamics, and more.

- **Audio Middleware**: Solutions like FMOD and Wwise provide advanced audio capabilities, including 3D sound, real-time mixing, and interactive audio.

- **Networking Middleware**: Photon, UNet, and RakNet are examples of networking middleware that simplify the implementation of multiplayer functionality and real-time synchronization.

- **AI Middleware**: Middleware such as Behavior Designer and Recast/Detour aids in creating complex AI behaviors and navigation meshes.

3. Advantages of Middleware Integration

Integrating middleware into your project offers several benefits:

- **Time and Cost Savings**: Middleware solutions save development time by providing ready-made functionality, reducing the need for in-house development.

- **Quality and Reliability**: Middleware is often developed and maintained by experts in their respective domains, ensuring high-quality and reliable performance.

- **Focus on Core Gameplay**: Leveraging middleware allows developers to focus more on core gameplay and unique features, rather than reinventing the wheel.

4. Challenges and Considerations

While middleware integration offers many advantages, there are some challenges and considerations to keep in mind:

- **Licensing Costs**: Some middleware solutions come with licensing fees, which can impact the project's budget.

- **Integration Effort**: Integrating middleware may require substantial effort and expertise to ensure it seamlessly fits into the project.

- **Compatibility**: Ensure that the chosen middleware is compatible with your target platforms and game engine.

- **Updates and Maintenance**: Regular updates and maintenance of middleware are essential to address issues and security vulnerabilities.

5. Code Example: Integrating Audio Middleware

Here's a simplified example of integrating an audio middleware solution like FMOD into a game engine:

```cpp
#include "FMOD/fmod.hpp"

// Initialize FMOD

FMOD::System* audioSystem;

FMOD::System_Create(&audioSystem);

audioSystem->init(512, FMOD_INIT_NORMAL, nullptr);

// Load and play a sound

FMOD::Sound* sound;

audioSystem->createSound("sound.wav",        FMOD_DEFAULT,
nullptr, &sound);

sound->setMode(FMOD_LOOP_OFF);

FMOD::Channel* channel;
```

audioSystem->playSound(sound, **nullptr**, **false**, &channel);

// Update audio system (call this in the game loop)

audioSystem->update();

Middleware integration involves more comprehensive setup and configuration, but this example demonstrates the basic process of initializing and using an audio middleware system.

6. Conclusion

Middleware and SDK integration can significantly enhance your game or graphics application by providing access to powerful pre-built solutions. However, it's crucial to carefully evaluate middleware options, consider licensing costs, and plan the integration process effectively to reap the benefits fully. When done correctly, middleware integration can accelerate development and lead to a polished and feature-rich final product.

Section 19.5: Testing and Quality Assurance

Testing and quality assurance (QA) are essential phases in game development to ensure that your game is free of critical bugs and delivers a smooth and enjoyable player experience. In this section, we will explore the significance of testing and QA in game development and the various aspects you need to consider.

1. Types of Testing

Game testing encompasses a wide range of activities, each serving a specific purpose:

- **Functional Testing**: Ensures that the game's features and mechanics work as intended. Testers check for issues such as gameplay glitches, control problems, and objective completion.

- **Compatibility Testing**: Focuses on verifying that the game runs smoothly on different hardware configurations, operating systems, and platforms. This includes testing on various devices for mobile and console games.

- **Performance Testing**: Evaluates the game's performance, including frame rate, load times, and resource usage. Performance testing helps identify bottlenecks and optimize game performance.

- **Security Testing**: Addresses potential vulnerabilities in multiplayer or online games, including cheating prevention, data protection, and network security.

- **Usability Testing**: Assesses the game's user interface (UI) and overall user experience. Usability testing helps improve menu navigation, controls, and player engagement.

2. Importance of QA

Quality assurance plays a crucial role in game development for several reasons:

- **Player Experience**: QA ensures that players have a smooth and enjoyable gaming experience, leading to higher player satisfaction and better reviews.

- **Bug Detection and Fixing**: QA teams identify and report bugs, glitches, and other issues, allowing developers to fix them before release.

- **Compatibility and Performance**: QA helps ensure that the game works on a variety of platforms and performs well under different conditions.

- **Reduced Post-Launch Issues**: Rigorous QA can prevent major issues and costly updates after the game's release, preserving the developer's reputation.

3. QA Process

The QA process typically involves the following steps:

- **Test Planning**: Define test objectives, scope, and testing methods. Create test plans and test cases.

- **Testing Execution**: Testers perform various tests based on the test plans, record issues, and provide feedback.

- **Bug Reporting**: Testers report bugs and issues to the development team using bug tracking tools.

- **Regression Testing**: After developers fix reported issues, testers perform regression testing to ensure that new changes do not introduce new bugs.

- **User Acceptance Testing (UAT)**: Some games involve UAT, where actual players test the game to provide feedback on gameplay and user experience.

4. Automation in QA

Automation tools and scripts are increasingly used in game QA to improve efficiency. Automated tests can quickly check for common issues, repetitive tasks, and performance benchmarks. However, not all testing can be automated, and manual testing by human testers remains crucial.

5. Code Example: Automated Testing

Here's a simplified example of an automated test script using a testing framework like Unity's Test Runner:

```csharp
using UnityEngine;

using NUnit.Framework;

public class GameManagerTests

{

[Test]

public void GameManager_StartsGameWithZeroScore()

{

GameManager gameManager = new GameManager();

gameManager.StartGame();

Assert.AreEqual(0, gameManager.GetScore());

}

[Test]

public void GameManager_IncreasesScoreOnCollect()
```

```
{

GameManager gameManager = new GameManager();

gameManager.StartGame();

gameManager.CollectItem();

gameManager.CollectItem();

Assert.AreEqual(2, gameManager.GetScore());

}

}
```

This code demonstrates two simple automated tests for a game's GameManager class, checking if it starts the game with a score of zero and increases the score correctly when items are collected.

6. Conclusion

Testing and quality assurance are integral parts of game development that ensure your game meets player expectations and functions correctly across various platforms. Effective QA processes, both manual and automated, help identify and resolve issues before they impact the player experience, contributing to a successful game launch. Prioritizing QA can lead to better reviews, higher player engagement, and overall success in the competitive gaming industry.

Chapter 20: Final Project: Advanced Game Demo

In this concluding chapter, we'll delve into the process of creating an advanced game demo that incorporates many of the concepts and techniques discussed throughout this book. This final project will serve as a practical application of your knowledge, allowing you to showcase your skills and creativity. Here, we'll outline the initial steps for designing the game concept and getting started on your advanced game demo.

20.1: Designing the Game Concept

Before diving into development, it's crucial to have a clear and well-defined game concept. Here are the key steps in designing your game concept:

1. Idea Generation

Begin by brainstorming ideas for your game. Consider the type of game you want to create (e.g., first-person shooter, role-playing game, platformer) and think about the genre, setting, and story.

2. Defining Gameplay Mechanics

Outline the core gameplay mechanics that will make your game unique and engaging. How will players interact with the game world, and what challenges or puzzles will they face?

3. Creating a Storyline

Develop a compelling storyline or narrative for your game. This could involve creating characters, a backstory, and plot twists that will captivate players.

4. Designing Levels or Environments

Plan the game's levels, environments, and maps. Consider the layout, visual style, and any special features or obstacles unique to each level.

5. *Art and Visual Style*

Decide on the art style and visual direction for your game. This includes character design, environmental assets, and overall aesthetics.

6. *Sound and Music*

Think about the audio elements of your game, including background music, sound effects, and voice acting if applicable.

7. *User Interface (UI)*

Design the user interface, including menus, HUD elements, and any on-screen prompts or information.

8. *Platform Considerations*

Determine the platforms your game will target. Will it be for PC, consoles, mobile devices, or a combination of these? Each platform may have unique requirements and constraints.

9. *Monetization Strategy (if applicable)*

If your game will be commercial, consider the pricing model (e.g., one-time purchase, free-to-play with in-app purchases) and any monetization features.

10. *Scope and Milestones*

Define the scope of your project and set milestones for development. This helps you stay on track and manage the project effectively.

11. Feedback and Iteration

Once you have a rough concept, seek feedback from peers or potential players. Use their input to refine and improve your game concept.

Remember that your game concept should be achievable within your skill set and available resources. While it's great to aim high, it's also essential to set realistic goals for your advanced game demo.

As you proceed with your final project, you'll implement advanced graphics techniques, realistic physics, AI behaviors, and more, all while following best practices for game development. This chapter sets the stage for your journey in creating a remarkable game demo that showcases your expertise and creativity. Good luck!

20.2: Advanced Graphics Techniques Integration

In this section, we'll delve into the integration of advanced graphics techniques into your final game demo. As you've learned throughout this book, advanced graphics play a pivotal role in enhancing the visual appeal and realism of modern games. Here, we'll explore some key techniques to consider integrating into your project.

1. Realistic Lighting: Implement advanced lighting models such as Physically-Based Rendering (PBR) to achieve lifelike material properties. Utilize image-based lighting (IBL) for accurate reflections and dynamic global illumination (GI) techniques for realistic indirect lighting.

2. Dynamic Shadows: Enhance the immersion by incorporating dynamic shadow techniques, including shadow mapping, cascaded shadow maps (CSM), or ray-traced shadows. These techniques will make objects cast accurate and visually appealing shadows in real-time.

3. Post-processing Effects: Integrate post-processing effects like bloom, depth of field, motion blur, and color grading. These effects can dramatically improve the visual quality of your game and create cinematic experiences.

4. Particle Systems: Create stunning particle effects for things like explosions, fire, smoke, and magic spells. Utilize GPU acceleration to handle large numbers of particles efficiently.

5. Advanced Materials: Experiment with advanced materials, including subsurface scattering for realistic skin, iridescent surfaces, and volumetric fog. These materials add depth and richness to your game's visuals.

6. Procedural Generation: Implement procedural techniques for generating terrain, vegetation, or even entire worlds. Procedural generation can provide an almost infinite variety of content for your game.

7. High-quality Textures: Utilize high-resolution textures, normal maps, and displacement maps to add intricate surface detail to your game's assets. Texture atlases and texture compression can help optimize memory usage.

8. Advanced Animation: Incorporate complex character animations, including inverse kinematics (IK), ragdoll physics, and facial animation. These animations enhance the realism and interactivity of your game.

9. Sound and Music Integration: Ensure that your game's audio complements its visuals. Implement 3D sound systems, spatialized audio, and realistic sound propagation to immerse players in the game world.

10. Optimization and Performance: Continuously optimize your graphics pipeline to ensure smooth performance, even on lower-end hardware. Techniques like level of detail (LOD) and occlusion culling can help achieve this.

11. VR/AR Integration (if applicable): If your game is designed for virtual reality (VR) or augmented reality (AR), ensure proper integration of tracking and input systems. Optimize rendering for VR headsets to maintain high frame rates.

12. Testing and Debugging: Rigorously test and debug your graphics implementations. Profiling tools and techniques will help you identify and resolve performance bottlenecks.

Remember that the successful integration of these advanced graphics techniques requires careful planning and implementation. Be prepared to iterate and refine your graphics as you work on your final game demo. By leveraging these techniques, you can create a visually stunning and engaging gaming experience that captivates players and showcases your skills as a game developer.

20.3: Implementing Realistic Physics

In this section, we'll focus on implementing realistic physics for your final game demo. Realistic physics simulation adds depth and immersion to games by accurately modeling the behavior of objects, characters, and the environment. Whether your game involves characters interacting with the physical world or objects responding to forces, physics plays a crucial role. Here, we'll explore how to integrate physics into your project effectively.

1. Physics Engine Integration: Consider integrating a physics engine like NVIDIA PhysX, Bullet, or Havok. These engines provide pre-built solutions for simulating physics interactions, including rigid body dynamics, collision detection, and character controllers.

2. Rigid Body Dynamics: Implement rigid body physics to simulate the movement and interactions of solid objects. Define collision shapes, mass, and friction properties for objects to ensure they behave realistically when subjected to forces.

3. Character Controllers: If your game involves characters, implement character controllers to handle character movement, including walking, running, jumping, and climbing. Consider adding features like crouching and prone positions.

4. Joints and Constraints: Use physics joints and constraints to create complex physical interactions between objects. This can include hinges, springs, ropes, and other mechanisms that add realism to your game world.

5. Collision Detection: Ensure accurate collision detection between objects in your game. Implement collision layers and masks to control which objects interact with each other. This is essential for preventing unintended collisions and improving performance.

6. Particle Systems: Integrate physics-driven particle systems for effects like sparks, debris, and fluid dynamics. These systems simulate the behavior of individual particles, creating visually appealing and realistic effects.

7. Vehicles and Physics-Based Gameplay: If your game includes vehicles or physics-based gameplay, model vehicle dynamics and physics interactions. Implement features like suspension systems, tire friction, and vehicle stability.

8. Ragdoll Physics: For characters or creatures in your game, implement ragdoll physics to simulate realistic responses to impacts and forces. Ragdoll physics can greatly enhance the believability of character animations.

9. Physics-Based Puzzles and Interactions: Design gameplay mechanics and puzzles that leverage physics. This can include puzzles that require players to manipulate objects, balance structures, or solve challenges through physics-based interactions.

10. Optimization: Optimize your physics simulations to ensure smooth gameplay performance. Consider using techniques like spatial partitioning, frustum culling, and LOD for physics objects.

11. Debugging and Testing: Implement debugging tools for physics, such as visualizing collision shapes, forces, and constraints. Use these tools to identify and resolve physics-related issues during development.

12. Integration with Graphics: Ensure that physics interactions are seamlessly integrated with your graphics engine. Objects should respond realistically to forces, collisions, and interactions, enhancing the overall visual and gameplay experience.

By incorporating realistic physics into your final game demo, you can create a more immersive and interactive gaming experience. Whether your game is focused on action, puzzles, or simulations, physics simulation adds depth and realism that can captivate players and make your game stand out. Remember to balance realism with gameplay fun and iterate on your physics implementations to achieve the desired player experience.

20.4: AI and Player Interactions

In this section, we'll delve into implementing Artificial Intelligence (AI) and player interactions in your final game demo. AI is a critical aspect of many games, allowing NPCs (Non-Player Characters) and enemies to behave intelligently and respond dynamically to the player's actions. Player interactions, on the other hand, involve the ways players can interact with the game world, NPCs, and objects. Let's explore how to create engaging AI and interactions for your game.

1. AI Architecture Selection: Choose an appropriate AI architecture for your game. Common options include behavior trees, finite state machines, and utility-based AI. The choice depends on the complexity of your NPCs' behavior.

2. NPC Behaviors: Define various behaviors for NPCs, such as idle, patrol, follow, and attack. Create AI states and transitions that allow NPCs to switch between these behaviors based on game events and player actions.

3. Pathfinding: Implement pathfinding algorithms to allow NPCs to navigate the game world intelligently. Algorithms like A are commonly used for efficient pathfinding.*

4. Decision-Making: Develop decision-making systems for NPCs to make choices based on their goals and the current game state. Consider factors like threat assessment, resource management, and player interactions.

5. Player Interactions: Create meaningful ways for players to interact with NPCs and the environment. This can include dialogues, trading, quests, and object manipulation. Implement interaction mechanics that enhance the player's immersion.

6. Dialog Systems: If your game includes dialogues, design a dialog system that supports branching conversations, choices, and character responses. Implement tools for easily scripting dialogues and managing character interactions.

7. Combat AI: If your game involves combat, design AI behaviors for enemies and allies. Implement combat tactics, evasion, and target selection algorithms to make battles engaging and challenging.

8. Dynamic Difficulty Adjustment: Consider implementing dynamic difficulty adjustment mechanisms that adapt the game's difficulty based on the player's performance. This ensures that players of varying skill levels can enjoy the game.

9. Emotional AI: For more immersive storytelling, explore emotional AI systems that allow NPCs to express emotions like happiness, fear, and anger. Emotional AI can enhance character depth and empathy.

10. Player Feedback: Provide clear feedback to players regarding AI behaviors and interactions. Use visual and audio cues to convey NPCs' intentions and responses.

11. Testing and Balancing: Rigorously playtest and balance your AI and interactions to ensure a fun and fair player experience. Adjust AI parameters, behavior probabilities, and interaction outcomes as needed.

12. AI Debugging Tools: Implement debugging tools for AI behavior. These tools can help you visualize NPC decision-making, detect AI bugs, and fine-tune AI behaviors.

13. AI Learning and Adaptation: Consider incorporating machine learning techniques for AI learning and adaptation. Reinforcement learning or neural networks can enable NPCs to improve their behaviors over time.

14. Performance Optimization: Optimize AI code and data structures to minimize performance impact. Use techniques like spatial partitioning for efficient AI updates in complex scenes.

15. Accessibility: Ensure that AI behaviors and player interactions are accessible to players with different abilities. Implement features like subtitles and customizable controls to accommodate a broader audience.

16. Documentation: Document AI behaviors and interactions thoroughly to aid in collaboration and future development. Clear documentation is valuable for maintaining and expanding your game.

By implementing AI and player interactions effectively, you can create a dynamic and engaging game world where players feel immersed and challenged. Whether your game leans towards storytelling, strategy, or action, AI and interactions play a pivotal role in shaping the player's experience. Invest time in designing and refining these aspects to deliver a memorable gaming experience in your final game demo.

20.5: Polishing and Final Thoughts

As you approach the completion of your advanced game demo project, it's crucial to focus on polishing every aspect of the game. Polishing goes beyond just bug fixing; it involves refining the game's visuals, audio, gameplay, and overall player experience to make it as impressive and enjoyable as possible. In this final section, we'll discuss the key steps for polishing your game and offer some closing thoughts.

1. *Visual Polish:*

- Ensure consistent art style and graphics quality throughout the game.

- Pay attention to details like character animations, particle effects, and environmental assets.

- Optimize textures and models for performance without compromising quality.

2. *Audio Enhancement:*

- Fine-tune sound effects and background music to match the game's atmosphere.

- Implement positional audio to enhance immersion.

- Test audio across various devices and adjust volume levels for balance.

3. *User Interface (UI) Improvements:*

- Create an intuitive and visually appealing user interface.

- Implement UI animations, transitions, and feedback for a polished feel.

- Ensure that UI elements are responsive and accessible.

4. *Gameplay Balance:*

- Playtest rigorously to identify and address any gameplay balance issues.

- Adjust enemy difficulty, item spawns, and progression to provide a satisfying challenge.

- Seek player feedback and iterate on gameplay mechanics as needed.

5. Bug Fixing:

- Thoroughly test your game for bugs, glitches, and crashes.

- Prioritize fixing critical issues that affect gameplay or stability.

- Create a bug tracking system to manage and prioritize bug reports.

6. Performance Optimization:

- Profile your game's performance and optimize code, shaders, and assets.

- Ensure smooth gameplay on a variety of hardware configurations.

- Optimize loading times and minimize frame rate drops.

7. Quality Assurance (QA):

- Conduct comprehensive QA testing to catch any remaining issues.

- Test on different platforms and devices to ensure cross-compatibility.

- Verify that all game mechanics work as intended and adhere to design specifications.

8. Localization:

- If your game targets international audiences, consider localization.

- Translate in-game text, dialogues, and subtitles into multiple languages.

- Ensure that localized versions are culturally sensitive and contextually accurate.

9. Accessibility:

- Make your game accessible to a wider audience by implementing accessibility features.

- Provide options for customizable controls, subtitles, and visual aids.

- Conduct accessibility testing with players who have disabilities.

10. Player Feedback:

- Gather feedback from playtesters and early players.

- Consider making adjustments based on player suggestions and preferences.

- Address common player complaints and frustrations.

11. Documentation and Tutorials:

- Document your game's features, mechanics, and design choices.

- Include tutorials or in-game tooltips to help new players understand the game.

- Make it easy for players to access help and instructions.

12. Marketing and Promotion:

- Plan your game's marketing and promotion strategy well in advance.

- Create marketing materials, trailers, and a website to generate interest.

- Utilize social media, gaming forums, and influencers to reach your target audience.

13. Release Planning:

- Plan a strategic release date that maximizes visibility and sales potential.

- Coordinate with distribution platforms and storefronts for a smooth launch.

- Prepare press releases and store descriptions to highlight your game's unique selling points.

In conclusion, the final phase of developing your advanced game demo is a critical one. The effort you invest in polishing your game will have a direct impact on how players perceive and enjoy your creation. Remember that a well-polished game not only provides a more enjoyable experience but also leaves a lasting impression on players and potential collaborators. So, take your time, iterate, and strive for excellence in every aspect of your game. Best of luck with your advanced game demo, and may it be a testament to your skills and creativity in the world of game development!

www.ingramcontent.com/pod-product-compliance
Lightning Source LLC
Chambersburg PA
CBHW021418150726
47989CB00001B/27